DESIGN STUDIO
2022 VOLUME 4

Design Studio Vol. 4 Working at the Intersection: Architecture After the Anthropocene is printed on Revive Offset Recycled 300gsm and 120gsm paper, FSC® Recycled 100% post-consumer waste. Papers Carbon Balanced by the World Land Trust. Printed with eco-friendly high-quality vegetable-based inks by Pureprint Group, the world's first carbon neutral printer.

© RIBA Publishing, 2022

Published by RIBA Publishing,
66 Portland Place, London, W1B 1AD

ISBN: 9781914124051
ISSN: 2634-4653

The rights of Harriet Harriss and Naomi House to be identified as the Editors of this Work have been asserted in accordance with the Copyright, Designs and Patents Act 1988 sections 77 and 78.

All rights reserved. No part of this publication may be reproduced, stored in a retrieval system, or transmitted, in any form or by any means, electronic, mechanical, photocopying, recording or otherwise, without prior permission of the copyright owner.

British Library Cataloguing-in-Publication Data

A catalogue record for this book is available from the British Library.

Commissioning Editor: Alex White
Assistant Editor: Scarlet Furness
Production: Sarah-Louise Deazley
Designed and typeset by Linda Byrne
Printed and bound by Pureprint Group Ltd
Cover image: Cave_bureau

While every effort has been made to check the accuracy and quality of the information given in this publication, neither the Author nor the Publisher accept any responsibility for the subsequent use of this information, for any errors or omissions that it may contain, or for any misunderstandings arising from it.

www.ribapublishing.com

About the Editors **V**

Acknowledgements **V**

Editor's Introduction: Beyond the Spaces of Speciesism
Harriet Harriss
and Naomi House **VII**

ARTICLES

A Brief Architectural History of Intersectionality
V Mitch McEwen **1**

Architecture is Dysphoric and Wants to Transition
McKenzie Wark **11**

Non-Binary Ecologies?
Harriet Harriss and Naomi House **21**

Loser Images: A Feminist Proposal for Post-Anthropocene Visuality
Joanna Zylinska **33**

Planetary Portals in the Upside-Down World
Casper Laing Ebbensgaard,
Kerry Holden and Kathryn Yusoff **40**

From Anthropocene to Biocene: Novel Bio-Integrated Design as a Means to Respond to the Current Biodiversity and Climate Crisis
Marcos Cruz and Brenda Parker **52**

Sitopia: A Landscape for Human and Non-Human Flourishing
Carolyn Steel **62**

PROFILES

A Troublesome Trail of Improvision Towards the Chthulucene
Kabage Karanja and Stella Mutegi **73**

For Landscapes of the Post-Anthropocene
Antón García-Abril and
Débora Mesa **81**

The Architecture of Analogous Habitats
Ariane Lourie Harrison **88**

CASE STUDIES

The Wilding of Mars
Alexandra Daisy Ginsberg **97**

Bat Cloud
Joyce Hwang **103**

In Between Landscape: Nvidia Headquarters
Walter Hood **109**

Final Word
Timothy Morton **117**
Contributors **122**
Recommended Reading **124**
Index **126**
Image Credits **129**

DESIGN STUDIO 2022 VOLUME 4

Working at the Intersection

Architecture After the Anthropocene

About the Editors

Professor Harriet Harriss (RIBA, FAIA, PhD) is a qualified architect and dean of the Pratt School of Architecture in Brooklyn, New York. Prior to this, she led the architecture research programmes at the Royal College of Art in London. Her teaching, research and writing focus on pioneering new pedagogic models for design education, and widening participation in architecture to ensure it remains as diverse as the society it seeks to serve. Dean Harriss has won various awards including a Brookes Teaching Fellowship, a Higher Education Academy Internationalisation Award, a Churchill Fellowship, two Santander Fellowships, two Diawa awards and a NESTA (National Endowment for Science, Technology and Art) Pioneer Award.

Naomi House is a designer, educator and writer. A Senior Lecturer in Interior Architecture and Design, and Research Coordinator at Middlesex University, London, she is an experienced academic who taught for many years in Critical and Historical Studies at the Royal College of Art, and previously at the Bartlett School of Architecture, UCL, London Metropolitan University and University of the Arts, London. Naomi's particular expertise is in the field of interiors using forensic methods as a strategy for exploring and questioning how objects, environments and their interactions can be analysed, interpreted and animated.

Acknowledgements

All books are acts of collectivism. We owe too many thanks to too many people, but particularly those closest to the bright burn of our pandemic-exacerbated struggles and triumphs with this text. We are especially grateful to Barry Curtis for donning the drag of mainstream critique, lingual legibility and grammatical housekeeping; to Vineeta Mudunuri for her invaluable help in collating the images and designing the website; to our commissioning editor, Alex White, who shared our commitment to the thematic ambitions of the book, without the assurance of comparable precedent; and to our assistant editor, Scarlet Furness, for managing the various intersecting components of the book with forensic attention. Extra special thanks go to V. Mitch McEwen, whose sagacious critique rightly highlighted the fundamental problem of white editors creating a platform for a discussion on environmental racism. Mitch is also responsible for a critical revision to the title, and consequently, this too should be credited to her.

And to our own critters, to whom we owe everything – Paul, Severn, Fiona, Pete, Holly, Martha, Bea, Sadie, Maud, Rudyard and Tank – thank you, and also, sorry. Our academic affair is over, at least for now, and we are coming home.

Editor's Introduction

Beyond the Spaces of Speciesism

Harriet Harriss and Naomi House

Images from the Anthropocene – Cracks between sheets of sea ice are called leads, as seen in this image of Arctic sea ice from the DMS instrument from a recent Operation IceBridge aerial survey.

When intersectionality is understood as a subset of identity politics, the ideological conflicts can seem distracting from more pressing global issues, such as the nested crises we call climate change and the radical new paradigms such crises require.[1] V Mitch McEwen

Functionally extinct koalas. Starving polar bears. Ecosystem collapse. Mass species die-off. Rapid desertification. Multi-dimensional flood risk. Arctic sea ice decline. Ocean acidification. Extreme weather mortalities. Speciesism. Climate feminism. Environmental racism. While these terms are becoming increasingly familiar, the sum of their meaning and impact is not. As academics, we are compelled to cite others in order to qualify our claims, and yet citations are a means through which 'established' scholarship offers an indiscreet code for reinforcing 'the establishment', and is generally understood to come from a set of imperialist, white and western economy-advantaging values systems. Consequently, 'citations' are the disciplinary and epistemological gabions that shore up divisive and elite privileging ideologies.

You do not need to own a naughty yet loving dog, binge on TV shows about octopus educators nor cheer on the interspecies adoptions that are routinely ranked among the most-watched YouTube videos to understand that humans are not the only creatures capable of empathy. Compassion, justice and ethics are elevated as virtues we have been encouraged to associate with the most altruistic aspects of our humanity, as many of the animal rights and ecological organisations evidence through how they choose to identify – *Compassion* in World Farming, Green*peace*, PETA (People for the *Ethical* Treatment of Animals), Union of *Concerned* Scientists, Earth *Alliance*, Earth *Justice*, *Friends* of the Earth, to name only a few – reinforcing the notion that caring for others – other humans or other species – is required in order to at least acknowledge, if not react to, their suffering.

Until relatively recently animal suffering, human suffering and climate collapse were studied separately, thanks to systems of partitioning knowledge into epistemologies (knowledge frameworks) and disciplines. As a direct consequence, policy responses have been inclined to speak to each 'problem' individually, but not collectively, or *intersectionally*. Instead, the many different struggles taking place are not challenged to compete, clash or cancel but, when combined, to *amplify*. Whether you are a koala burning alive in an Australian bushfire,[2] a farmer starving to death in Madagascar[3] or a 60-year-old Black woman in Brooklyn dying in a heatwave,[4] intersectionality explains why these experiences of climate collapse are not only related, but statistically likely to be more acute than if you were a koala in a city zoo, a farmer in Canada or a white woman living at the gentrified end of the same block in Brooklyn, but with the means to afford air-conditioning. As editors of this book, we acknowledge that any text seeking to make a contribution to the discourse surrounding *intersectionality* carries all kinds of contextual misapprehensions and socio-cultural appropriations that could do more harm than good. There is a messy edge between offering a platform for other voices, and the imperialism(s) and narcissism(s) of curatorial control implicit within academic writing. Intersectionality, when used as a device for contemplating architecture after the Anthropocene, risks the conflation of the needs of cuddly koalas with human suffering, and in doing so, obscures the true extent of environmental racism. As McEwen puts it:

'The proliferation of koalas and polar bears in descriptions of environmental collapse designate a human, as well – one who might be a conservator or protector, a figure who might allocate resources, rather than a person attacked or hunted. What ecological politics would emerge from thinking of the animal world as an extension of whiteness? Where are the sharks, bears, and vultures in these narratives – animals that trouble our forms of human congregation in ways that are often violent?'[5]

Shifting our attention to the anthropocentrism element of the book's thesis and, more generally, the identity-indifferent tropes we have observed within much ecological philosophy, neoliberal thinking has created a circuit-break on our ability to truly confront the ways in which our privilege correlates directly with another's exploitation or harm, by insisting that compassion can be both objective (meaning we observe, we feel something, but we don't act) *and* subjective (meaning we connect deeply with the feeling, and in doing so, supposedly debilitate ourselves from acting).[6] Both of these responses suggest that any kind of *acting*, any kind of reasonable attempt to intervene, will do little to impact the situation. In this sense the articles and case studies included here all assume some agency in the face of overwhelming inertia.

Today's social, political and environmental scientists and cultural theorists are already jostling to supersede what constitutes an *Anthropocene* with, predominantly, a *Capitalocene*,[7] which links ecological crisis to the logic of capitalism; a *Chthulucene*,[8] whereby composites of multi-species tell stories within conditions of planetary precarity, but not yet planetary collapse; or a *Technocene*, in which humans harness techno-utopianism to self-anaesthetise against the horrors of impending climate catastrophe – a strategy that architect Bjarke Ingels best illustrates by declaring his intention to 'prove that a sustainable human presence on planet Earth is attainable with existing technologies'.[9] In fairness to Ingels, renouncing the very infrastructures that provide techno-utopianists with an open mic to begin with would require not only humility, but a willingness to admit that the inequality and injustice that exists between members of the same species is precisely why white, male, northern-hemisphere species-narcissists who think they know better than (Mother) Earth are given any air time at all!

So, while a meaningful or effective response to the climate crisis caused during and/or by the Anthropocene remains unresolved, the transition into *post-anthropocentrism* by critical theorists is neither a dereliction nor a denial of what is taking place, but more a means to highlight that not all humans experience climatic collapse equally because not all humans are valued equally. This book exists because discussions about the future of architecture are contingent on the future existence of the planet, and has a particular resonance for architects, whose task it is to construct and create habitation. This book *needs* to exist because until issues of social injustice are acknowledged to be politically, economically and environmentally embedded in climate collapse, we will not find effective ways to halt, if not reverse, the deepening crisis.

In schools of architecture in the UK and elsewhere, students continue to be (falsely) assured that 'inclusive' design – a term that is far too simply addressed through legislation and building regulation – can legitimately focus exclusively on creating environments for humans and humans alone. This under-interrogated approach further liberates post-anthropocentric architecture from addressing the consequences of anthropocentrism, allowing it to become the quintessential typological broom cupboard for the many droids, distribution warehouses, drones, telecommunications networks and data stores full of digital versions of human actions that are, ostensibly, non-human. In order to determine what might constitute other architecture(s) after the Anthropocene, this book invites the reader to imagine, rage, rail, protest, contest, channel, dream and envision from a position of humility, equity and in some instances experiential fury. It is only

Images from the Anthropocene – Bandipur National Park wildfire, Karnataka, India, 2019. It is estimated that the fire extended across approximately 10,920 acres in five days.

'Christ's Descent into Hell', c. 1550–60, Hieronymus Bosch, Metropolitan Museum of Art, New York. Doomsday scenarios abound in existing responses to impending climate catastrophe.

Working at the Intersection: Architecture After the Anthropocene

by evidencing how multiple species can co-exist and even co-habit, and by designing spaces for interspecies extended families that rehabilitate and restore, that architects can take the first step towards earning both a professional and a planetary future.

Let us return to the story of the Black woman, living in Brooklyn, who died during a heatwave due to a lack of access to air-conditioning and ambient shade in a street devoid of trees – one of the numerous examples of environmental racism that pervade our newsfeeds. Let's be clear – climate collapse does not discriminate; rather, the legacy of American slavery and enduring racism within the US – a situation reflected globally – creates a system of inequality magnification that disadvantages specific demographics. Without environmental justice, there can be no social justice. Without social justice there can be no spatial justice. And, as the Covid-19 pandemic has served to illustrate, zoonotic infections reveal that the threshold between humans and animals is fragile and fast-evolving, highlighting the need to refocus architects away from designing the *spaces of speciesism* if we want to survive.

This book seeks to explore how interactions involving sexism, racism, classism, homophobia, isolation and environmental catastrophe are entirely interdependent, and that the solution to one cannot be found without confronting the other.[10] Consequently, we seek to expose blinkered perspectives currently dominating architectural education and professional practice, setting the table for a more inclusive engagement of the role of architecture in a global environment circumscribed by pandemic, climate change and conservative politics.

Part philosophy, part pedagogy, part practice and part provocation, in essence this volume's utility traverses and, hopefully, aligns design studio to history and theory. However, in truth, this book is also part petition – a pathetic plea to the generations hereafter whose negative-sum inheritance imposes upon them the obligation of working out how to pilot a Noah's Ark populated by perpetrators paired with their victims (bearing in mind that the perpetrators have their own architectural solutions – 'doomsday' bunkers in the US; an apocalypse retreat in New Zealand.[11]
In fact we would contend that 'survivalism' is one of the most prominent enemies of intersectionality). In pointing to architecture after the Anthropocene, the book pushes the reader towards contemplating what a *post-architecture* might look like and involve.

The book itself is divided into three sections – Articles, Profiles and Case Studies. The articles in particular operate as provocations, offering cross-disciplinary insights and positions in relation to the wider narrative. In the first, pivotal article, 'A Brief Architectural History of Intersectionality', V. Mitch McEwen expands upon Kimberlé Crenshaw's originating thesis, offering a critical framework through which both the title and contents of this volume might be read. McEwen's thesis establishes intersectionality as a mechanism which frames our understanding of the built environment – 'Intersectional work analyses the relationships of spatial segments and layers through the experiences of those who intersect and cross'[12] – challenging the totalising narratives of conservative environmental politics and eradicating human-centred thinking, to embrace an architecture of assemblages that is open and inclusive.

McKenzie Wark's contribution, 'Architecture is Dysphoric and wants to Transition', posits the end of architecture, speculating upon the invention of what she terms 'kainotecture' – a kind of framework for inhabitation that no longer separates human life from any other life form. Her speculations overlap into our own thesis on 'Non-Binary Ecologies', where we consider the dissolution of the nature/culture divide and discourse on the meaning and application of queer ecology. Joanna Zylinska's article, 'Loser Images', returns us to the core of post-anthropocenic thinking and contemplates the operation of visuality within this. Her degraded images destabilise the Cartesian view of the world with man at its centre, 'decoupling sight from a bipedal human body and dispersing it across the environment'.[13] In their 'Planetary Portals in the Upside-down World', Casper Laing Ebbensgaard, Kerry Holden and Kathryn Yusoff examine what they describe as 'the geo-social exchanges and affective architectures of extraction' through the trope of the portal as a conceptual device that 'connects seemingly unconnected geographies', exposing in the process 'the racialised logics of extractive capitalism'.[14]

Marcos Cruz and Brenda Parker's article, 'From Anthropocene to Biocene', interrogates the new materialisms that the Anthropocene has necessitated. Their thesis hinges on the intersection of living and semi-living 'entities' within architecture. This hybridisation of the natural and the synthetic establishes an extended architectural ecology in which the fabric of our built environment is infinitely modifiable and renewable. Carolyn Steel's essay, 'Sitopia', proposes food as the basis for a new kind of economy for a future beyond the

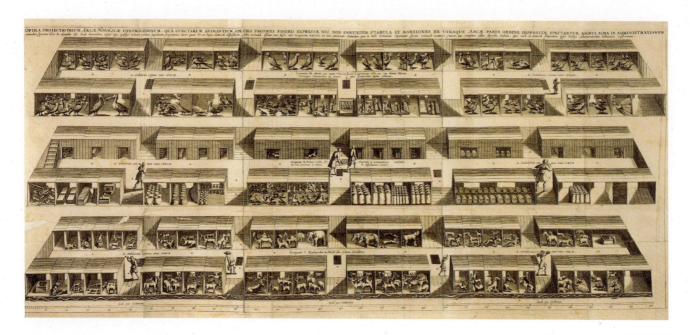

Artistic impression of internal view of Noah's Ark, showing the animals housed in their compartments over three decks. The animals and goods depicted here are stored as cargo.

Anthropocene. The landscape(s) which we inhabit, in order to sustain all life on this planet will need to value nature, and in particular food as the 'most potent symbol … of our commonality'.[15]

Part two of the volume moves us into the Profiles, with three exemplars from practice that address some of the wider impacts of the Anthropocene on how we conceive our environment. Cave_bureau's 'The Anthropocene Museum' operates as 'a site of enquiry' that 'reframes [the Anthropocene] through an African vantage point'.[16] Here 'museum' is a contested trope in which narratives of colonial and post-colonial struggle are played out, with the 'Anthropocene' itself as direct consequence of imperialist tactics. Ensamble Studio's 'Ca'n Terra' or House of the Earth is a serendipitous encounter with the subterranean landscape, made visible through the excavation and exploitation of the land. Using point-scan technology, Ensamble document this found space, capturing its 'overwhelming beauty'[17] as a precursor to producing a kind of hybrid architecture, in collaboration with the landscape rather than in control of it. The third building profile depicts Harrison Atelier's 'Pollinators Pavilion' – a project that seeks to challenge our understanding of what a post-human landscape might be. This analogous habitat recognises the complex challenge of species loss and how we might make room for non-human lifeforms in designing for a bio-diverse future.

The final section details three projects that further challenge our understanding and perception of an architecture of the post-Anthropocene. Alexandra Daisy Ginsberg's 'The Wilding of Mars' is depicted in an exhibition from 2019. Rather than invoking narratives of human colonisation of extra-terrestrial landscapes, this case study contemplates the surface of Mars as 'a repository for the mechanism of life'.[18] Here plants are seen to adapt to the specific atmospheric conditions of this alien landscape, offering a strange and incongruous vision of a new world where non-human life takes over. 'Bat Cloud' from Ants of the Prairie mirrors Atelier Harrison's building profile in the previous section in that it offers a habitat for non-human lifeforms – in this instance, bats. The project is a prototype that recognises the symbiotic relationship between different lifeforms within an urban context. Rather than symbolising the control of nature, here the city is understood as part of nature's habitat. The final project presented is Hood Design Studio's Nvidia Headquarters in Santa Clara, LA – a set of buildings and spaces that are responsive to both the climate and topography of the California landscape. Here is an architecture that makes the most of testing site conditions – exacerbated by rapid climate change – prefiguring an approach to making inhabitable environments that are adaptable to multi-species inhabitation.

The final contribution to this book comes in the form of a last word from Timothy Morton, who contemplates 'Playful Seriousness versus Serious Playfulness Or, Socialism versus Facism'. Within this construct 'playful seriousness' suggests an approach to the future that is creative, open and suggestive, whereas 'serious playfulness' is constrained, unimaginative and ultimately sterile. While inversions of this kind can be effectively deployed to trigger a form of proto-empathy in those who otherwise lack it: Put yourself in my shoes? How would you feel if you were the ant you just killed with bug spray? Such inversions, or indeed any form of polarisation of gender, colour, class, sexuality, ability, language, origin or national identity, cannot expect to elicit a meaningful response. Under these circumstances, creativity and openness are not available to all. Perhaps rendering this inequity obsolete is a place for architects to start.

1. V Mitch McEwen, 'A brief architectural history of intersectionality', *Working at the Intersection – Architecture After the Anthropocene*, Harriet Harriss and Naomi House, eds., London, RIBA Publishing, 2022, pXIV.
2. 'Hundreds of koalas feared burned alive in out-of-control bushfire near Port Macquarie', *The Guardian*, 30 October 2019, https://www.theguardian.com/australia-news/2019/oct/30/hundreds-of-koalas-feared-burned-alive-in-out-of-control-bushfire-near-port-macquarie.
3. Kaamil Ahmed and Rivonala Razafison, 'At least 1m people facing starvation as Madagascar's drought worsens', *The Guardian*, 10 May 2021, https://www.theguardian.com/global-development/2021/may/10/at-least-1m-people-facing-starvation-madagascar-drought-worsens.
4. Ese Olumhense and Clifford Michel, 'Looking for relief as summer heat wave hits black and brown neighborhoods hardest', *The City*, 15 September 2021, https://www.thecity.nyc/health/2020/7/29/21347387/new-york-city-summer-heat-wave-black-neighborhoods-pandemic.
5. V Mitch McEwen, 'A brief architectural history of intersectionality', pXIV.
6. Individualism and competition are the focus of right-wing/neoliberal thinking, and remain popular with many western electorates. In particular the erosion of welfarism and resistances to socialism are evident in the 'common sense' (Conservative/Republican) attributes of personal responsibility, freedom of choice and self-actualisation – and, ironically of course, most evangelical forms of Christianity. Popular emphases on 'wellbeing' and contemplation, which serve the attainment/perfection of self, remain at the forefront of such thinking. Philosophers such as Henry David Thoreau in the US and John Stuart Mill in the UK set the tone for this in the nineteenth century. According to Mill: 'The only freedom which deserves the name is that of pursuing our own good in our own way, so long as we do not attempt to deprive others of theirs', (John Stuart Mill, *On Liberty*, first published in 1859) – but with no real sense of the interrelatedness of privilege and impoverishment. Indeed, the notion of 'trickle down' implies that by serving your own ends you are somehow benefiting others.
7. Jason W Moore, 'Name the system! Anthropocenes and the capitalocene alternative', 9 October 2016, https://jasonwmoore.wordpress.com/2016/10/09/name-the-system-anthropocenes-the-capitalocene-alternative.
8. Donna Haraway, *Staying with the Trouble – Making Kin in the Chthlulucene*, Durham and London, Duke University Press, 2016, p2.
9. India Block, 'Masterplanet is Bjarke Ingels' plan to redesign Earth and stop climate change', *Dezeen*, 27 October 2020, https://www.dezeen.com/2020/10/27/bjarke-ingels-big-masterplanet-climate-change-architecture-news.
10. This expands on the scholarship of Carol J Adams, author of *The Sexual Politics of Meat* (1990) and *The Pornography of Meat* (2003), which link 'species' oppression to gender oppression. She argues that the objectification of women and animals follow similar patterns: both the 'fairer' sex and the four-legged are sexualised, dehumanised and finally abused. Similarly, Donna Haraway's scholarship highlights the relationship between misogyny, anthropocentrism, sadism and modern humanism (as captured in her early scholarly deconstruction of primatology in *Primate Visions* (1989)), which provides the theoretical basis and a segue to the environmental racism scholarship of Bullard (2001), Chevis (1986), Westra (2001) and Holifield (2013), among others.
11. Mark O'Connell, 'Why Silicon Valley billionaires are prepping for the apocalypse in New Zealand', *The Guardian*, 15 February 2018, https://www.theguardian.com/news/2018/feb/15/why-silicon-valley-billionaires-are-prepping-for-the-apocalypse-in-new-zealand.
12. V Mitch McEwen, 'A brief architectural history of intersectionality', pXIV.
13. Joanna Zylinska, 'Loser Images', p32.
14. Casper Laing Ebbensgaard, Kerry Holden and Kathryn Yusoff, 'Planetary Portals in an Upside-Down World', p40.
15. Carolyn Steel, 'Sitopia: A Landscape for Human and Non-Human Flourishing', p62.
16. Cave_bureau, 'The Anthropocene Museum', p72.
17. Ensamble Studio, 'Ca'n Terra or House of the Earth', p80.
18. Alexandra Daisy Ginsberg, 'The Wilding of Mars', p96.

Editor's Introduction: Beyond the Spaces of Speciesism

A Brief Architectural History of Intersectionality

V Mitch McEwen

Introduction to intersectionality

For the past three decades the Black feminist notion of intersectionality has extended from civil rights jurisprudence to activism, political rhetoric and scholarship throughout the humanities.[1] Architecture, however, has remained wilfully ignorant of these ideas. Architecture's overwhelming dedication to a euro-centred mapping of knowledge and technical notions of the planetary form a protective buffer against scholarship or activism informed by Black feminism. This volume, replete with innovative meditations on the Anthropocene and its aftermaths, announces a void where a Black feminist architectural theory should have already been. Working at the intersection anticipates a mode of work on the horizon for architecture and the built environment, broadly. Intersectionality indicates a mode of analysis, a method of reading and critique. The methods do not yet fully present themselves in our field. Yet, I hope there is a possibility to draw things together in this vacuum.[2] This article endeavours to create a directly architectural engagement with intersectional scholarship by tracing an architectural history of intersectionality. This brief architectural history of intersectionality proceeds from a close spatial reading of Kimberlé Crenshaw's 'Demarginalizing the Intersection of Race and Sex: A Black Feminist Critique of Antidiscrimination Doctrine, Feminist Theory and Antiracist Politics',[3] generally considered the foundational text for the notion of intersectionality and its role in critical race theory. Through an architectural reading of Crenshaw's case-law references, the twentieth-century industrial architect Albert Kahn gets entangled in the emergence of intersectionality, by way of an assembly plant in St. Louis. With reference to a recent Forensic Architecture project in Louisiana, I conclude by (intersectionally) reading the post-plantation logic of industrial assemblage along the Mississippi River and its physical threat to Black women and the planet.

When intersectionality is understood as a subset of identity politics, the ideological conflicts can seem distracting from pressing global issues, such as the nested crises we call climate change and the radical new paradigms such crises require. Faced with priorities around subjectivity or the planetary, architecture would, of course, responsibly choose to focus on the latter – including questions of carbon, ecosystemic collapse, nature and the broader rubric of the post-human. We live in an era that demands urgent transformation.

However, an architectural reading of Crenshaw's intersectionality finds different matters at stake in the very notion of intersectionality. It is important to note that Crenshaw's legal scholarship highlighted the intersection of race and sex not in order to critique discrimination, but to critique *antidiscrimination doctrine*, *feminist theory* and *antiracist politics*.[4] Within Crenshaw's analysis, the very spaces of modernity – juridical, economic, architectural and otherwise – generate the terrain in which intersectionality becomes legible and necessary. How, then, might an architectural reading of Crenshaw's legal argument extend the intersectional critique to *ecological doctrine*, *queer architectural theory* and *planetary politics* of the Anthropocene? Developing all these avenues is beyond the scope of this article. However, by developing an architectural reading of this significant Crenshaw text and its sites, I hope that this article may serve as a prompt and even a foundation for others to pursue these intersectional critiques in the field.

Intersectionality presents urgent questions for the post-humanist ambitions in environmental design. Specifically, in what ways does ecological work centre whiteness? In the encounter between human and non-human, in what ways is that human prefigured as white or male? Related to this, in the absorption of Black feminist politics into environmental work, in what ways does centring whiteness operate also through the animal as an extension of the Black subject? The proliferation of koalas and polar bears in descriptions of environmental collapse designates a human, as well – one who might be a conservator or protector, a figure who might allocate resources, rather than a person attacked or hunted. What ecological politics would emerge from thinking of the animal world as an extension of whiteness? Where are the sharks and vultures[5] in these narratives – animals that trouble our forms of human congregation in ways that are often violent?

This article cannot fully address these questions, as relevant as they may be for the discipline today. I do, however, return to questions of the planetary in conclusion, teasing out an intersectional planetary politics in recent collaborative work of Forensic Architecture and local organisers RISE St. James in Louisiana. Through their 2021 project Environmental Racism in Death Alley, Louisiana I read the industrial logic of the assembly plant across time, back to the plantation and forward through the life cycle of plastic. In the context of this ongoing activism outside of New Orleans, Black women exist within post-plantation industrial space as residents, but in a hybrid sense that I relate to the hybridity of civil rights claimants in Crenshaw's analysis. Both this hybridity and its erasure undergird the logic of toxic emissions and industrialisation of former plantations. The following analysis, then, traverses the assembly plant, plantation, sugar mill, and plastics factory – a grouping that defies 'typology' but coheres and repeats in relationship to Black women and across vast geographies where modernity assembles itself.

Critical race theory and modernity

Kimberlé Crenshaw introduced the concept of intersectionality in a legal essay published in 1989 titled 'Demarginalizing the Intersection of Race and Sex: A Black Feminist Critique of Antidiscrimination Doctrine, Feminist Theory and Antiracist Politics'.[6] She shows that judges have been able to throw out civil rights cases filed by Black women based simply on the impossibility of Black women representing any one experience of discrimination.

Underlying this conception of discrimination is a view that the wrong which antidiscrimination law addresses is the use of race or gender factors to interfere with decisions that would otherwise be fair or neutral.[7]

Using three legal cases as the basis of analysis, Crenshaw shows how the judicial system fails to recognise Black women as having civil rights claims. The fantasy premise of neutrality erases Black women's claims by centring whiteness as the standard for sex discrimination and maleness as the standard for race discrimination.

Crenshaw, as a legal theorist, focuses on case law. The first of three cases that Crenshaw analyses is *DeGraffenreid v. General Motors*, a civil rights case of 1976. The judge in *DeGraffenreid* found that five Black women could not challenge their employment termination as a civil rights violation, due to the mixing of sex discrimination and racial discrimination in their claims. Crenshaw demonstrates that this case and the ruling point to a larger and deeper bias towards whiteness and maleness, beyond one judicial opinion. This bias towards single and separable factors of experience extends through the logic of the Civil Rights Act. Crenshaw's argument operates on both a theoretical and a practical level. It undoes the distinction between (legal) theory and (civil rights) practice. Theoretically, she argues against uni-dimensionality, which is to say the entire metric system of the juridical process. She critiques the spatial order of civil rights jurisprudence.

Much of Crenshaw's argument takes the form of a calculus of vectors and neutral states. To the extent a neutral state presumes some unraced or unsexed person, it presumes whiteness and maleness. In addition, civil rights law and jurisprudence operate through presumptions of distinct and separable factors distorting the neutral state.

The point is that Black women can experience discrimination in any number of ways and that the contradiction arises from our assumptions that their claims of exclusion must be unidirectional.[8]

The contradiction that Crenshaw mentions is effectively between civil rights law and the lived experience of Black women. Not only does the system privilege whiteness and maleness as defaults, but it presumes that any discrimination must be unidirectional to become operable within civil rights claims. Black women experience multiple directions of discrimination in ways that cannot be easily parsed.

Within the unidirectional rubric that privileges whiteness and men as neutral, Black women could only be read as hybrids.

Discrimination against a white female is thus the standard sex discrimination claim; claims that diverge from this standard appear to present some sort of hybrid claim.[9]

This pattern of producing and expelling hybrids can be read as a hallmark of modernity. Modern systems suppress their collaborations with non-modern materials and technologies. Modern infrastructures reinforce the distinction between operation and maintenance, even when such distinctions are counterproductive.[10] As Bruno Latour argues in 'We Have Never Been Modern', modernity repeatedly purifies and hybridises, but only acknowledges purification processes as modern.

What separates the modern from the non-modern in Latour's analysis is not the scale or intensity of the purification and translation processes, but the horror around the hybrid.

Moderns do differ from premoderns by this single trait: they refuse to conceptualize quasi-objects as such. In their eyes, hybrids present the horror that must be avoided at all costs by a ceaseless, even maniacal purification.[11]

In Latour's formulation, quasi-objects and quasi-subjects appear as quasi only because the principles for classifying entities register mediation as disturbance.[12] Hybrids and quasi-objects facilitate the modern work of mediation (application, assembly, research and development, activism). Yet, modern institutions privilege the work of purification (pure science, pure materials, pure profit, pure sex discrimination). The expulsion of Black women that Crenshaw tracks at the level of civil rights can be understood as the work of modernity, as modern as the Corvettes assembled in the plant or the architecture of the plant itself.

Double separation
While Crenshaw focuses on legislation and jurisprudence, it is possible to read the events of the cases that Crenshaw cites as architectural events. As an architectural reference, the DeGraffenreid case can be analysed spatially as not only (legal) citation but (work) site. The corporate defendant in the case does not exist without the architecture of the assembly plant. It is important not to render the assembly plant as a type,[13] as this would reproduce the problems of privileged defaults and centres that Crenshaw criticizes. The assembly plant, itself, then, requires an intersectional reading. Would it be far-fetched to imagine that the unidirectional and neutralising logic at work in the modern jurisprudence of *DeGraffenreid v. General Motors* could also be analysed through the architecture of the assembly plant complex? What would become legible in the spatial logic of the assembly plant when we read it through the claims and experience of Black women?

The case defendants in *DeGraffenreid v. General Motors* are listed as 'GENERAL MOTORS ASSEMBLY DIVISION, ST. LOUIS, a corporation, et al.'. The assembly division mentioned in the case title occupied an assembly plant in north St. Louis. The work of parsing and then hybridising is also the work of the assembly plant. In order for a body to be assembled it has to have been previously disassembled. Materials and parts need to have been produced through processes of purification. An assembly plant is defined by a process, and vice versa. Through complexes such as the assembly plant, a 'series of substitutions, displacements and translations mobilize peoples and things on an ever-increasing scale'.[14] Latour charts this incomplete double work as work that happens in modern, as well as non-modern (pre-modern or post-modern), societies.

Within the assembly plant and its multiple levels, the modern topology of narrow lines of force meets the bureaucracy and the marketplace.[15] The St. Louis plant in question, similar to the Chevrolet plant in Flint Michigan (below), includes levels above for engineering and operations. The additional levels above the assembly floor provide surface area for the bureaucracy of the assembly process – the operations of assembly on paper, including accounting and payroll. The sectional relation of above and below is critical. As Latour outlines, such a sectional separation enables double separations.

The double separation is what we have to reconstruct: the separation between humans and nonhumans on the one hand, and between what happens "above" and what happens "below" on the other.[16]

Whereas Latour traces this argument through the constitution (separation of powers) and the laboratory (representation of power), the assembly plant stages such separation of powers as productivity and efficiency, along with separation of humans and non-humans, whites and non-whites, men and women.

The bureaucracy above the assembly floor is not agentless. The bureaucracy above the shop floor requires labour embedded in local interaction and social exchanges. As Latour notes, 'The myth of the soulless, agentless bureaucracy, like that of the pure and perfect marketplace, offers the mirror-image of the myth of universal scientific laws.'[17] The operations bureaucracy requires women to do much of its work. The layers can be diagrammed as shown left.

The all-white space of engineering and operations includes women as agents of the bureaucracy. The all-male space of the shop floor includes Black bodies intermingled with machines.

To consider Crenshaw as a counter, extension and predecessor to Latour's ideas of the modern – to in some ways replace the constitution with the assembly plant

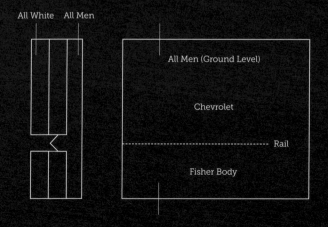

This diagram is indebted to Jeannette Moore, a retired Ford accountant in Detroit who described to me her unique ability, as a Black woman, to move between plant levels to communicate and manage disputes – between accounting and workers on the autobody shop floor.

Microplastics, tiny nurdles and plastic debris in a rockpool, Gower Peninsula, Swansea, Wales.[18]

– demands an intersectional spatial analysis *within* logics of assembly. This would mean developing an attunement to striations and thresholds – any architecture that filters which subjects may be permitted to enter – as well as to climate in all its effects (including racism and sexism).[19]

Albert Kahn

Perhaps only Albert Khan could have designed an industrial complex with an interior large enough and multi-storeyed enough to absorb and expel Black women from the core of global capitalist industry. As we know from Crenshaw's argument, Black women experience the intersection of multiple dimensions of exploitation. Once Black women were absorbed as employees they revealed the racism, sexism and exploitation at the core of the assembly plant logic. This architectural history of intersectionality discovers Albert Kahn to be an architectural agent embedded in the legal case that Crenshaw cites.

Beginning with a Fisher Body plant in 1922, Albert Kahn designed the St. Louis assembly plant for GENERAL MOTORS ASSEMBLY DIVISION, ST. LOUIS, the defendant in *DeGraffenreid v. General Motors*. Kahn continued to work on the project through 1966, following General Motors' acquisition of the Fisher corporation. Using a slew of custom-engineered systems, from the reinforced structural members to the material finishing, Kahn designed the plant as a complex capable of accreting and aggregating.

What if the question of who can enter worked its way backwards through the entire design process? Rather than thinking of types, typologies or authors, we could then think of this design and repetition through inquiries of access – access to techniques, geometry, patterns, codes, material, structural logics, labour practices. This would make the work of Albert Kahn significant to study not as a type of building but as an archive of access to industrial techniques.[20] Indeed, architecture itself could become legible as a set of practices that assemble, an assembly plant of structural, material, spatial and social realities.

An assembly plant is a place of multiple climates, distinct spaces, mezzanine levels, racks and bodies, gantries, curtains and other custom spatial assemblages. The Kahn plant in question sprawls over 275,000 square metres.[21] It is different from a factory.[22] A factory might make one thing over and over. It digests materials. It can easily operate via remote control. An assembly plant requires numerous material variables and processes of transformation. It constitutes a final step before public consumption. The assembly plant is the place where the fibreglass body becomes the Corvette.

The plant at the crux of this analysis, the St. Louis plant that could legally expel all Black women employees as late as 1976, assembled Corvettes. The car model may seem arbitrary, but it is not. The Corvette, the first American-made sports car, required fabrication of a body out of composite materials that were unfamiliar to GM manufacturing processes. The Fisher Body plant remained referenced in Kahn's plans for decades, despite Fisher Body, the corporation, having been acquired and merged into Chevrolet/GM in 1926.[23] Kahn's plan retains the separation of the Fisher Body plant from Chevrolet with two rectangular areas cleaved by a rail line. The two volumes are connected at one hinge behind the rail line. The plant itself retained and assembled former bodies of assembly.

The hybrid is the Corvette, an automobile conceived as a body, a morphology of speed requiring fibreglass materials to form. It is a car as body. It is a hybrid body-car that required all sorts of hybrid techniques and 'trial and error' to assemble.[24] As the car required a hybridisation of techniques, so did the building itself. Kahn's architectural production for the plant fills multiple boxes, each containing multiple folders of drawing sets.

Box 19:
Chevrolet Motor Company, Floor over Court, Fisher Body Section, St. Louis, MO, (1954–1956), Job No. 1088-F&G (4 folders)
Chevrolet Motor Company, Oven Supports and Enclosure on Roof, Fisher Body Section, St. Louis, MO, (1955–1956), Job No. 1088-H (2 folders)

Box 20:
Chevrolet Motor Company, Three Story Addition to "B" and "D" Buildings, St. Louis, MO, (1960–1961), Job No. 1088-K (5 folders)
Chevrolet Motor Company, Final Process Addition and Car Loading Building, St. Louis, MO, (1961–1962), Job No. 1088-L (7 folders)
Chevrolet Motor Company, Alterations and Additions to Plant for Increased Storage, St. Louis, MO, (1962–1963), Job No. 1088-M (5 folders)
Chevrolet Motor Company, Corvette Building Additions, St. Louis, MO, (1963–1964), Job No. 1088-N (3 folders)
Chevrolet Motor Company, Building Additions at West End of Passenger Assembly Line, St. Louis, MO, (1964), Job No. 1088-P
Chevrolet Motor Company, First Floor Building Addition, St. Louis, MO, (1966), Job No. 1088-R [25]

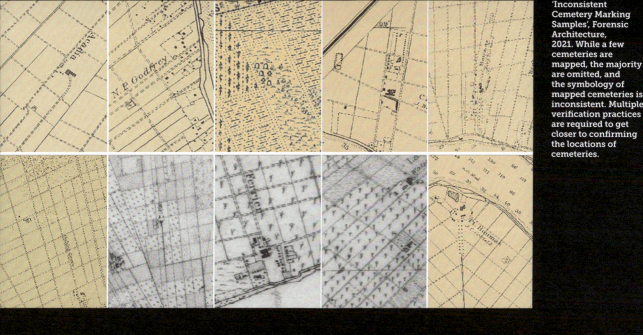

'Inconsistent Cemetery Marking Samples', Forensic Architecture, 2021. While a few cemeteries are mapped, the majority are omitted, and the symbology of mapped cemeteries is inconsistent. Multiple verification practices are required to get closer to confirming the locations of cemeteries.

In the drawing set titles alone, we can read outdoor courtyards converting to interiors, interiors expanding and grounds re-surfacing, roofs becoming outdoor production spaces and offices multiplying in levels. These architectural acts of assembly and disassembly accompanied the hybrid assembly of the Corvette, through the years that the first Black women employees were hired there. It is within this flux of hybrids that Black women were absorbed and expelled, as hybrid labourers with no rights as such.

Death by sugar

A plantation is equal parts industrial facility [sugar mill], farm, prison [slave quarters], death camp, and luxury estate [big house].[26] Forensic Architecture

What if we understood modern industrial space as a continuation of prior facilities and assemblies, including the plantation? This would disrupt the Taylorist myth of efficiency, the visual metaphor of smooth operations, or the synecdoche of machinic organisation. Analysis of the industrial as plantation would, rather, open possibilities to understand the relationship between landscape and industry as one not of factory versus nature, but spatial parts of a whole economy – an assemblage of spaces that operate together to assemble and disassemble popula-

Forensic Architecture published 'Environmental Racism in Death Alley, Louisiana Phase I Investigative Report' on July 4, 2021.[27] The publication date alone signals the intent of the project to be read as a critical assessment of a national pattern, not only one local to Louisiana. The fourth of July is the date that the United States celebrates Independence. The report's analysis of industrialised environmental racism along Louisiana's Petrochemical Corridor situates the history of industrialisation within the plantation, asking 'If toxic air is a monument to slavery, how do we take it down?'[28]

The answer to that question lies, oddly enough, with the ancestors. Experts from the UN Human Rights Watch have visited this stretch of the Mississippi River to investigate the human rights threats constituted by the concentration of over 150 oil refineries, and plastic and chemical plants.[29] RISE St. James, a Louisiana organisation led by Black women, commissioned Forensic Architecture to develop a predictive spatial method for identifying the locations of nineteenth-century Black cemeteries before industry breaks ground on further intensification and expansion. The organisers of RISE St. James reside on free Black land adjacent to the plastic industry that has replaced the nineteenth-century sugar mills. Their commissioning of Forensic Architecture brilliantly leverages Louisiana state law's comprehensive protections claim to protect the living. Protection is critical because, in the proximity to the plastics industry, the residents of St James have elevated cancer rates and other demonstrable harm from the toxic industrial climate. RISE St. James commissioned Forensic Architecture not only to locate the cemeteries for tactical purposes, but also to gather evidence in support of their claims for accountability and reparations. This even included measuring and visualising the racism in the air.[30]

To locate the Black cemeteries, Forensic Architecture deployed an assemblage of tactics, from topographical data, to historical mapping, to anthropological analysis. They intersected knowledge of burial rituals and plant life with spatial data.

Enslaved people were interred in uncultivated lands at the back of the plantation, at the edge of the Cypress forest. As cultivated fields expanded, cemeteries became isolated islands adrift in seas of cane.[31]

The historical mapping reveals that expanding industrial plants steadily homogenised many of these topographical anomalies that marked the burial sites, erasing them from the historical record of the ground over the last half of the twentieth century. The industrial logic renders these sites as anomalies or landscape hybrids, while the intersection of Black rituals and resistance charges these sites as critical agents within larger ongoing claims to reparations, human rights and planetary futures.

The impacts of petrochemical production in Louisiana's Petrochemical Corridor extend to many of the Black residents, but, of course, do not end there. The petrochemical industrial projects currently contested by RISE St. James include Formosa Plastics' 'Sunshine Project' – a 3.5-square mile plastic nurdles production complex.[32] Plastic nurdles, the colourful pre-production unit of plastic manufacturing, comprise a small percentage of the plastic entering oceans. However, they have an outsize impact on marine habitats, due to their resemblance to fish eggs and other marine life, and their capacity to absorb pollutants.[33] RISE St. James, a coalition organised and led by Black women descended from enslaved residents of former plantations, in contesting the immediate threat to themselves, their children and their gardens, also contest a wider system that spills death-inflicting materials across species and environments at a planetary scale.

I conclude with Crenshaw's tactical argument for intersectional work. The intersectional, she argues, accords with bottom-up approaches to change.

"[B]ottom-up" approaches, those which combine all discriminatees in order to challenge an entire employment system, are foreclosed by the limited view of the wrong and the narrow scope of the available remedy. If such 'bottom-up' intersectional representation were routinely permitted, employees might accept the possibility that there is more to gain by collectively challenging the hierarchy rather than by each discriminatee individually seeking to protect her source of privilege within the hierarchy.[34]

Within the intersectional work of Black cemetery claims, there is no conflict between ecosystem and residents, or preservation and economy, labour rights and human rights. RISE St. James, led by the most marginalised and impacted, supported by Forensic Architecture and human rights experts, demonstrates the capacity of the bottom-up collective to challenge the petrochemical hierarchy. Even prior to the outcome of the legal contestation to stop further construction, this collective work challenges the industrial hierarchy by revealing the ways this hierarchy founds itself on plantation logics and territories.

Intersectionality as an architectural modality extends to the planetary. The plantation's sugar mill becoming plastic plant, like the assembly plant, gives us the models to understand striated and segmented spaces that assemble and disassemble products, people and landscapes. Intersectional work analyses the relationships of spatial segments and layers through the experiences of those who intersect and cross. This differs conceptually and geometrically from work that privileges those at the centre, even when ostensibly expanding and democratising a central experience. The work of intersection troubles the assumption that changing society can be imagined by erasing segments and making them uniform. From the intersection, we can see the formalism of smooth edges, single surfaces and landscaped parametricist urbanisms as the fantasy of a centre that never ends, an endless big house. An architectural history of intersectionality requires analysis of assemblages. Reading Kimberlé Crenshaw as an architectural thinker gives us a way out of the trap of the non-racialised post-human, as well as the formalism of the single surface (green or otherwise). In the exclusion of Black women from civil rights claims, we can map the means by which universal logics can deny access to humanity. To quip a mash-up of Bruno Latour and Barbara Smith: We Have Never Been Human, But Some of Us Are Brave.[35]

'Industrial Expansion', Forensic Architecture, 2021. Multiple layers of public data reveal the ongoing sell-off of land along Death Alley, including residential land that is home to 'fenceline' communities.

'Whitney Plantation – Anomalies', Forensic Architecture, 2021. The Black descendant community of Wallace traces its ancestry to several plantations under threat by the pending construction of an industrial grain elevator. Forensic Architecture have identified several anomalies within high probability zones of the Whitney and adjacent plantations.

1   This is especially true within the digital humanities and gender studies. A by no means exhaustive list includes: Patricia Hill Collins and Sirma Bilge, *Intersectionality*, Polity Press, 2016, 2nd edition, 2020; Barbara Bordalejo and Roopika Risam, *Intersectionality in Digital Humanities*, Arc Humanities Press, 2019; Amber Johnson and Benny LeMaster, *Gender Futurity, Intersectional Autoethnography: Embodied Theorizing From the Margins*, Routledge, 2020; Emily Grabham, Davina Cooper, Jane Krishnadas and Didi Herman, *Intersectionality and Beyond: Law, Power and the Politics of Location*, Abingdon, Routledge-Cavendish, 2008; Helma Lutz. 'Intersectionality as method', *DiGeSt. Journal of Diversity and Gender Studies*, vol. 2, no. 1–2, Leuven University Press, 2015, pp39–44.
2   I am hinting at the ways that this text (over-)relies on Bruno Latour, especially 'Drawing things together' and *We Have Never Been Modern*. The latter text begins the story of modernity with the airless vacuum. See Bruno Latour, 'Visualisation and cognition: Drawing things together', *Avant: Trends in Interdisciplinary Studies*, vol. 3, no. T/2012, pp207–60 and Bruno Latour, *We Have Never Been Modern*, trans. Catherine Porter, Cambridge, MA, Harvard University Press, 1993.
3   Kimberlé Crenshaw, 'Demarginalizing the intersection of race and sex: A black feminist critique of antidiscrimination doctrine, feminist theory and antiracist politics', *The University of Chicago Legal Forum*, no. 1, 1989, pp139–67.
4   Crenshaw, title (emphasis mine).
5   The vulture appears in the declaration of independence for Haiti, *Liberté ou La Mort*, as a figure for the French, following a description of the colonial French as *ce peuple bourreau* and *machinateurs de nos troubles et nos divisions*. Jean-Jacques Dessalines, 'Liberté ou la mort' [Haitian declaration of independence], 1 January 1804, CO 137/111, The National Archives of the United Kingdom, p4. Thank you to Anjuli Fatima Raza Kolb for the reference.
6   Crenshaw, 'Demarginalizing the intersection of race and sex'.
7   Ibid., p151.
8   Ibid., p149.
9   Ibid., p145.
10 For more on modern infrastructure as purification and maintenance see V Mitch McEwen, 'Profound modernity', *e-flux Architecture*, https://www.e-flux.com/architecture/positions/156858/profound-modernity, October 2017.
11 Latour, *We Have Never Been Modern*, p112.
12 Latour, *We Have Never Been Modern*, 'This beautiful order is disturbed once the quasi-objects are seen as mixing up different periods, ontologies or genres', p73.
13 Or, worse, 'typology'.
14 Latour, *We Have Never Been Modern*, p84.
15 Here I am considering the assembly plant as one form of 'gigantic rationalized organizations' that rely upon 'a new topology that makes it possible to go almost everywhere, yet without occupying anything except narrow lines of force.' Latour, *We Have Never Been Modern*, p120.
16 Ibid., p13.
17 Ibid., p121.
18 'Plastic "nurdles" found littering UK beaches', BBC News, 17 February 2017, https://www.bbc.com/news/uk-
19 I am using the term 'climate' here to evoke Christina Sharpe's work on weather and climate. A longer study would hesitate here on the relationships between interior climatic controls and hybrid labour. 'At stake here is not recognizing antiblackness as total climate. At stake, too, is not recognizing an insistent Black visualsonic resistance to that imposition of non/being.' Christina Sharpe, *In the Wake: On Blackness and Being*, Durham and London, Duke University Press, 2016, p21.
20 See Charles K Hyde, 'Assembly-line architecture: Albert Kahn and the evolution of the U.S. auto factory, 1905–1940', *IA. The Journal of the Society for Industrial Archeology*, vol. 22, no. 2, 1996, pp5–24.
21 'The main plant alone is on three floors and encompasses 3,157,000 square feet of space.' John McGuire, 'FOCUS: St. Louis. Bold rebirths for industrial dinosaurs', *New York Times*, 7 May 1989, https://www.nytimes.com/1989/05/07/realestate/focus-st-louis-bold-rebirths-for-industrial-dinosaurs.html.
22 'The word factory generally refers to a production site where a specific item is produced, whereas a plant refers to a site where a specific process takes place … A plant usually means a place where things are not usually constructed, rather it is an area or building, such as where fresh water is produced by purification, or sewage is disposed, or where grain is milled into flour.' Econo Service Agency, 'Why is a factory called a plant?', https://econoagency.org/useful_information/930.
23 Olivier Germain and Didier Chabaud, 'Theory and history, remarks from Fisher Body – General Motors case', *Conference: Academy of Management Annual Meeting*, https://www.researchgate.net/publication/200139117_Theory_and_History_Remarks_from_Fisher_Body-General_Motors_Case, August 2008.
24 'Plant manager William Mosher noted that assembling fiberglass bodies was challenging for line workers, managers and engineers alike. Mosher remembered, "At the beginning, it was a trial and error method that seemed torturously slow until we got the knack of it."' MotorTrend, 'A look at the three Corvette assembly plants', https://www.motortrend.com/features/1907-look-three-corvette-assembly-plants.
25 Bentley Historical Library and Albert Kahn Associates, Albert Kahn Associates records, Albert Kahn Associates, https://quod.lib.umich.edu/b/bhlead/umich-bhl-87445?byte=210048315;focusrgn=C01;subview=standard;view=reslist.
26 Forensic Architecture, 'Environmental racism in Death Alley', video, minute 21, https://forensic-architecture.org/investigation/environmental-racism-in-death-alley-louisiana.
27 Forensic Architecture, 'Environmental racism in Death Alley, Louisiana phase I investigative report 4 July 2021', https://content.forensic-architecture.org/wp-content/uploads/2021/07/Environmental-Racism-in-Death-Alley-Louisiana_Phase-1-Report_Final_2021.07.04.pdf.
28 Forensic Architecture, p4.
29 UN News, 'Environmental racism in Louisiana's "Cancer Alley", must end, say UN human rights experts', 2 March 2021, https://news.un.org/en/story/2021/03/1086172.
30 'RISE St. James have commissioned Forensic Architecture to gather evidence in support of their claims for accountability and reparations and develop a predictive method for identifying the locations of antebellum Black cemeteries before industry breaks ground. Our investigation draws focus to elements of the climate of racism that linger just beyond the threshold of visibility: the lethal chemical agents that pervade the air, and the traces of erased Black cemeteries that cling to the surface of the earth.' *Forensic Architecture*, p4.
31 *Forensic Architecture*, video, minute 25.
32 *Forensic Architecture*, p3.
33 Fidra, 'The great nurdle hunt: Tackling worldwide nurdle pollution', *The Problem*, 2021, https://www.nurdlehunt.org.uk/the-problem.html.
34 Crenshaw, 'Demarginalizing the intersection of race and sex', p145.
35 Gloria T Hull, Patricia Bell Scott and Barbara Smith, *All the Women are White, All the Blacks are Men, But Some of Us are Brave: Black Women's Studies*, Old Westbury, NY, Feminist Press, 1982.

Kisho Kurokawa, Nakagin Capsule Tower, Shimbashi, Tokyo, Japan, 1972. A mixed-use development consisting of capsule apartments and offices, the building is an example of the Japanese Metabolist school – a postwar architectural movement which intersected modern movement ideas around megastructures with the growth characteristics of biological organisms.

Architecture is Dysphoric and Wants to Transition

McKenzie Wark

Architecture has a relation to itself and the world, but it is one that causes it considerable unease.

Let's take architecture at its most rudimentary, as a structure that creates a stable relation between an interior and an exterior, that keeps something out and something in. An architecture subordinates the vector of movement into and out of a particular location to the maintenance of the membrane that separates the inside from an outside. An architecture makes, and regulates, an interiority. There will be movement across its membrane, but those movements appear secondary to the persistence of the border.

An architecture, as an enclosure of an interiority, presupposes an exteriority that is greater than it, but which is to some extent unknown and unmarked. An architecture vets and regulates the vectors across its membrane in either direction – incoming and outgoing – but is mostly concerned with moments of passage across its perimeter, not with the origin or destination of the vector that crosses it. And yet an architecture assumes this 'elsewhere' exists. The vector comes to its doorstep and leaves by the back door to somewhere else as well. That other place has to be there, somewhere, but for architecture it is without qualities.

In the root of the word itself – architecture – is the notion of some sort of stability. The structure doesn't collapse. Like in the biblical parable, architecture is built on rock, not on shifting sand. It is stable also in this other sense: that there's a consistent relation between an interiority and an exteriority. With the added qualification that the interiority is specific, located somewhere, has definite capacities to regulate the passage of any vector across its bounds. That regulation may not be absolute, but it is definite. Whether what flows along the vector is solid, liquid or gas, architecture regulates passage across the border of an interiority. It regulates the passage of humans and other forms of life, and also, more generally: passages of energy and information.

These vectors come from somewhere and go somewhere, before and after passing in and out through the portals of architecture. But that somewhere can remain unknown. Architecture deals in partial totalities, separated off from a world that only needs to be vaguely known. Architecture limits what it knows about exteriority to what it needs to know to ensure a stable relation to it. A relation that maintains an interior from which certain forms of life are excluded. It presupposes an exterior where other forms of life exist.

Let's call this maintenance of a semi-permeable membrane with a relation to an outside a *metabolism*. It comes from a Greek word meaning change, but in this context gestures specifically towards kinds of regulated change. Those familiar with the history of architecture will already know of the Japanese Metabolist school. My use of the term here is a little different, although I do want to acknowledge what for me is the enduring beauty of its members' pioneering work. However, like practically all architecture that we know, their work was created within the Holocene geologic era. It was not yet widely known that the intensity of planetary extracting and building, and the venting of waste back out along unspecified vectors, would in themselves bring about an end to the entire Holocene epoch.

This is the hard part for thinking about 'architecture', in the broadest sense of the word. The thing that causes a certain unease. It is architecture itself which put an end to the relative stability of the Holocene epoch and tipped the entire planet towards the instability of the Anthropocene. This is meant as a provocation, of course. It might be more useful to say that the endless, ever-expanding circuit of capitalism is what is destroying the Holocene and its conditions of life.[1] But then we might want to think about how architecture as we now know it is inseparable from capitalism. This architecture is coterminous with capitalism as a property form.

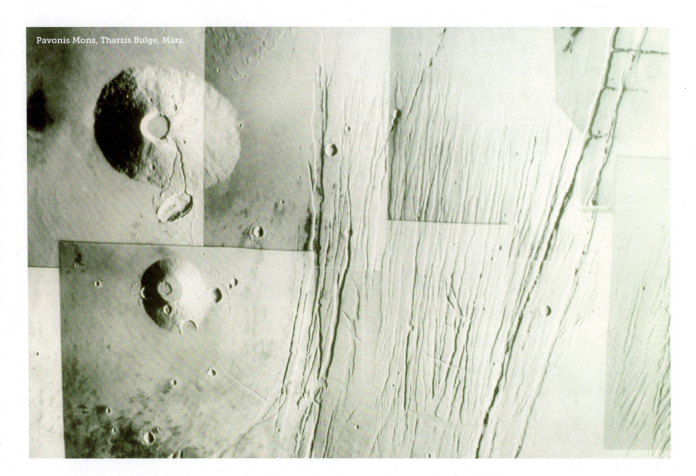

Pavonis Mons, Tharsis Bulge, Mars.

What if no such stable relations were possible anymore? What if the Anthropocene signalled the end of architecture and called for some other concept of built form altogether? Maybe architecture has to transition to something else. Let's call it *kainotecture*, from *kainos*, which among other things might mean something new, or more exactly a qualitative break into a different kind of time. That's what the Anthropocene is in relation to the Holocene: a change in geological time.

Kainotecture might be a way of thinking about building which does not create an interior that separates human life from other kinds of life. Kainotecture might have a different history to architecture. Most of what anyone knows about built form is from the Holocene. But there are exceptions. For instance, Australian Aboriginal life most likely has consistencies that stretch back to the late Pleistocene period. One might begin gathering not just a knowledge of particular building habits, but general practices of being in the landscape from there, although one has to acknowledge also how fraught it is for a colonising and extractivist culture to learn from that which it attempted, but failed, to destroy.[2]

There may also be practices that anticipate kainotecture. These might be found in the margins of existing architectural history and thinking, at least by marking out the limits of what architecture as a discipline encloses. I'll just mention a few with which I'm familiar. Perhaps for architecture to transition it would help to think about some other thing. One would be visionary proposals that critique and negate the limits of building practices that exist within capitalist modes of production.

For instance, *Constant's New Babylon*, which presupposes the abolition of private property and wage labour.[3] Looked at in terms of elevation, it stratifies all of planetary built space, with automated production buried underground, as the base layer. Circulation, at ground level, is the mediating layer. Above it is a network of malleable structures. The spatial arrangement is a literal version of Marx's schematic understanding of any mode of production: economic base determines cultural and political superstructures.[4] The abolition of private property erases the distinction between private and public space and the need for stable property relations in real estate. The nomadic denizens of New Babylon are free to wander anywhere, change anything. Their only struggle is with boredom.

Constant's work is a visionary critique of architecture but not quite a step towards a kainotecture. The whole of human life is enclosed as one metabolism. But Constant still imagines New Babylon as enclosed and separate from the world. It's a vision for one species only – the human. It is the limit case of a planetary modernism.

A step beyond that, in more ways than one, might be in the radical science-fiction imaginary of Kim Stanley Robinson.[5] Whether on Earth or on Mars, Robinson imagines built forms that are at the edge of plausibility, but which take account of just how different form might have to become if the human is to endure – even if in Robinson the human becomes other things as well: many-gendered, and more. Robinson imagines a post-human, multi-species world, and understands permeability between worlds as key to any possible kainotecture.

But what of actual, real-world examples? Here there might be more upon which addresses instability as an aspect of kainotecture than permeability. One example I've used in the past is the kainotecture of war. Paul Virilio famously wrote about the bunkering of Europe by the Nazis, and its inability to hold back the vectors of permeation of attack by the Soviet Union, the United States, Britain and their allies.[6] The kainotecture that made possible the Normandy invasion, complete with temporary artificial harbours, is an extraordinary undertaking in temporary, unstable building.[7]

There's something all too tempting, though, in the language of war as a way of thinking about the Anthropocene. What if, instead, we thought about the language of care? For one thing, that shifts perspective away from the kind of masculinist sensibility of examples drawn from the built forms of war. I want to go a little further than that and imagine kainotecture from the point of view of care networks, such as the 'covens of care' specific to trans women.[8]

Batterie de Longues-sur-Mer, German bunker, Normandy, France, 1943–4. The bunker formed part of Germany's Atlantic Wall, but was captured during the D-Day landings on 7 June 1944.

Left: G. H. Davis, The Aircraft Carrier of Ice, The Illustrated London News, 1946. A diagram showing the details of the top secret plans for an aircraft carrier, HMS Habbakuk, a giant aircraft carrier made largely of ice and wood-pulp.

Opposite: The aftermath of Hurricane Katrina, New Orleans, Louisiana, 4 September 2005. The flooded streets of New Orleans are seen in this aerial view.

14   Working at the Intersection: Architecture After the Anthropocene

The first thing a lot of trans women will ask about our fate should our world collapse is: how will we get our hormones? There's already the beginnings of an interesting vein of speculative trans literature that makes exogenous hormones a key to imagining mid-apocalyptic scenarios.[9] But perhaps the apocalyptic is not a good genre for thinking about kainotecture, or the Anthropocene, as it tends to imagine that forms of mutual aid and covens of care collapse when there is a break in the temporal order, when if anything the reverse might be the case. In a disruption, care networks sometimes spring into action.[10]

Some caveats are important here, particularly for non-trans readers. Firstly, trans people are not the only ones whose existence depends on external, technical, medical forms of support. One thing we can learn from disability studies is that at some time, in some way, we all do.[11] The focus on trans people just picks out a specific case about which I happen to know something.

The other caveat is that trans-ness is not identical to the current forms of western, medicalised life. We have always existed, and in many different ways. Even in modern, western worlds a lot of us have depended, and may still depend, on forms of mutual care outside of the formal medical and technical world.[12] Still, it has to be stressed that many of us function much better in the world with access to the tools to hack our own endocrine systems and to modify the metabolism of sex within our bodies.

Like most groups of people with a rare and specific form of embodiment, we are usually the best source of knowledge and support about what it means to be one of us in the world. Reading what the 'experts' have said about us, and passed off as knowledge, can fill a transsexual with rage.[13] The design of any possible kainotecture would surely benefit not just from consulting various kinds of the 'other-embodied', but actually handing some of the process over to us.

There are things it is invasive to ask someone about, which rules out mere consultation anyway. Surely most non-trans people ought to know by now not to ask us 'have you had the surgery?' Even as a trans woman, I hesitated in asking other trans women about this when I was contemplating bottom surgery for myself. Once I summoned up the courage to ask another about her orchiectomy. It's a simple outpatient procedure to remove the testicles, where most testosterone is produced in bodies assigned male at birth. I'm glad I asked: one of the reasons she gave me for getting it done is that when civilisation collapses and access to hormones is disrupted, she does not want her body to revert to its masculine form. That answer stunned me and got me thinking about what kainotecture will mean for 'girls like us'.

After Hurricane Katrina, Sybil Lamb spent some time in the disaster area, and has written a fictional account of that experience.[14] Like in a post-apocalyptic

book or movie, characters live in a lawless state and raid abandoned stores and pharmacies. Fortunately, hormones are a cheap and plentiful industrial pharmaceutical product. Such a measure, however, could only be temporary.

I was at a rave with a trans friend when the power went out. We stopped dancing and just stood there. 'What are we going to do,' I asked, 'when civilisation ends, and we can no longer get our beats or our hormones?' She gave me a level look and declared: 'We're going down with the ship.' Whether we can endure many of the remaining futures or not, at least as we currently live our lives, is an open question. But perhaps we have something to contribute to thinking about worlds that others might still get to inhabit. One thing the trans experience offers is a way to think about metabolism, given that hacking a metabolism to make it one we can endure is exactly what being trans is about.

Thanks to Jules Gill-Peterson's pathbreaking work, we now have some ways to think about how the plasticity of the metabolism of the body came to be thought of in the postwar period through experiments in the somewhat questionable field of sexology.[15] Scientists found that bodies existed in a range of states that did not fit a neat binary of sexes. Through experimentation they also discovered how easily modified the sex of the body was. The (western, institutionalised) distinction between 'biological' sex and social 'gender' arose out of a need to stabilise what 'male' and 'female' meant. Contrary to many received ideas on this, it was gender as social role that was posited as a clear and consistent binary, because sex within the flesh was just too plastic and variable a ground for a consistent model of the sexed body.

Consequently, both intersex and transsexual bodies were to be treated in ways that brought the metabolism of the sexed body in line with a social role that was taken as fixed and highly binarised. The artifice of medical and technical interventions into the regulation of sex in metabolic flesh was to bring wayward, plastic flesh into line with social norms. Bodies could be designed to function according to social desires – which in the early postwar period took the form of historically specific, racially coded, heterosexual gender norms. The racialised dimension of sexology is key. The white body was special in its degree of plasticity. The non-white body was somehow too intractable. The plasticity of metabolism at all levels – the body, the building, the city – was somehow a special attribute of white science.

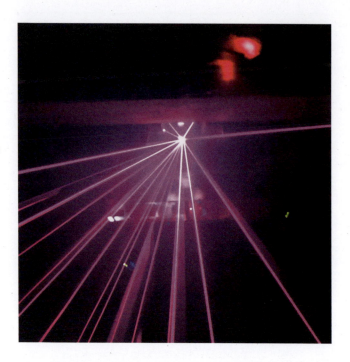

This marks part of the limit of even visionary work like *Constant's New Babylon*. He does not stop to wonder if the rest of the world wants this plastic megastructure imposed on top of it. New Babylon just spreads everywhere like utopian imperial kudzu in his imagination. The most advanced, meaning most western, technics is the most plastic. It is one of the boldest Marxist visions for built form, but all the same a relentlessly Eurocentric one.

There's a school of thought within Marxism that focuses on a concept Marx was developing in the margins as he worked on *Capital*: that of *metabolic rift*. John Bellamy Foster was perhaps the first to draw attention to it.[16] From his readings to the work of soil scientist Justus von Liebig, Marx concluded that capitalist agriculture was not sustainable. It interrupted the metabolic process that connected a human population to agriculture. Trace elements such as nitrogen and phosphorus, essential to life, were not being replenished. The shift in population from country to city, and to wage labour there, created a rift in the phosphorus and nitrogen cycles. Bellamy and others have generalised Marx's insight as a way to think of climate disruption as metabolic rift on a planetary scale. The displaced element in this scenario is not phosphorus or nitrogen – it's carbon.[17]

While Marx's thinking on metabolic rift has been in his writings for anyone to pick up since the late nineteenth century, it has only been in the postwar period that Anglophone interpreters of Marx

Opposite: McKenzie Wark, Rave.

Below: Morwell open-cut coal mine, Victoria, Australia, 2000.

Architecture is Dysphoric and Wants to Transition

have highlighted metabolism as a concept. Jordy Rosenberg offers the startling suggestion that it was the popularisation of 'metabolism' in fields such as sexology that indirectly led to this reading.[18] For Rosenberg, there's a trans perspective within Marxism that can connect the politics of knowledge around trans healthcare to the politics of knowledge around the Marxian critique of political economy, because both are in significant ways centred on concepts of metabolism, which became a popular concept across fields around the same time.

I want to extend that provocation to thinking about architecture, or what it might transition towards in an era of metabolic rift – kainotecture. A trans perspective might at one and the same time think about how on the bodily scale, as well as that of the building, the city and the planet, metabolic states are out of whack. Their regulation presupposes an elsewhere. The vectors both in and out of body, building or city come from and go to an elsewhere that has to remain undefined, blank, empty. But that is no longer possible, when at the planetary scale the regulation of all other metabolic envelopes of the human is adding up to one gigantic metabolic rift. There's no elsewhere at the planetary scale.

There's a note of caution that the trans experience with interventions into metabolism introduces into this line of thinking, however. Ours are bodies that were treated as requiring interventions to 'fix' the regulation of the sex of the body – but healing that metabolic rift subordinated our bodies to patriarchal and racist ideologies of ideal genders.

With those caveats in mind, I want to risk a kind of metaphorical substitution, between the trans body and the planetary scale, but suggesting that both experience a kind of *dysphoria*, perhaps even in both cases gender dysphoria. Not all trans people experience dysphoria, but it is very common. As the name implies it's the opposite of euphoria; a kind of unease, dread or alienation. Gender dysphoria is an unease with the body's experience of itself in the gender it has been assigned. It is not merely discomfort with gender as social role, but a deep dread within the flesh about the body's sex.[19]

One could think of the dysphoric body as profoundly troubled by the signals it is receiving from both within and without. It's not unlike a metabolic rift. The body can't go on without modifying its relation to an outside. One can go on for a long time ignoring the signs of gender dysphoria or hesitating to do something about it. A term some trans people use for a person on the edge of coming to realise that their dysphoria is telling them to transition is an 'egg'.

What if the world itself, at least as some of us experience it, was in an egg state? What if there was a planetary dysphoria, where the signals are causing a deep unease but the will is not there to come out and do something about it? The planet itself might need to transition to another gender. What genders do planets come in? Nobody knows, as there is just this one with which most of us are familiar. But then trans people don't always know what gender they are heading towards – just that there's one they have to get out of before it kills them.

Kainotecture has to respond to more than one limit condition of architecture. It might point towards a built form that can no longer assume a stable relation to an outside. And it has to recognise the signals traversing its borders, along one vector or another, pointing to the dysphoric planet upon whose shifting sands or rising tides it is attempting to build. And then also: it has to keep track of the vector that traverses its walls more intently. There's no longer an outside to built form. It can no longer be where anything comes from or where it goes.

Architecture has to recognise its dysphoric state, and transition, even if there's no knowing what it might have to transition into. But that what being trans is like. It might even have moments of euphoria. Here one might look to Constant or Robinson just as a couple of partial precedents. It might have moments enduring violence, and there the kainotecture of past wars might be illuminating. But it might also have moments of collective care and becoming.

Opposite: McKenzie Wark, Brooklyn Liberation for Black Trans Lives, 13 June 2021.

1. Jason Moore, ed., *Anthropocene or Capitalocene?*, Oakland, CA, PM Press, 2016.
2. Elizabeth Povinelli, *Geontologies: A Requiem for Late Liberalism*, Durham, NC, Duke University Press, 2016.
3. Mark Widgery, *The Hyper-Architecture of Desire: Constant's New Babylon*, Rotterdam, 010 Publishers, 1998.
4. Karl Marx, 'Preface' to *A Contribution to the Critique of Political Economy*, New York, International Publishers, 1971.
5. Kim Stanley Robinson, *2312*, New York, Orbit, 2013.
6. Paul Virilio, *Bunker Archaeology*, New York, Princeton Architectural Press, 1997.
7. McKenzie Wark, 'From architecture to kainotecture,' *eflux journal*, https://www.e-flux.com/architecture/accumulation/122201/from-architecture-to-kainotecture, 5 April 2017.
8. Precarity Lab, *Technoprecarious*, London, Goldsmiths Press, 2020.
9. Torrey Peters, *Infect Your Friends and Loved Ones*, Brooklyn, 2016; Gretchen Felker-Martin, Manhunt, New York, Tor Books, 2022.
10. Rebecca Solnit, *A Paradise Built in Hell*, New York, Penguin, 2010.
11. Dan Goodley, *Disability Studies: An Interdisciplinary Introduction*, Thousand Oaks, CA, Sage, 2016.
12. Hil Malatino, *Trans Care*, Minneapolis, University of Minnesota Press, 2020.
13. Susan Stryker, 'My words to Victor Frankenstein,' *GLQ*, no. 3, 2014, pp237–54.
14. Sybil Lamb, *I've Got a Timebomb*, Brooklyn, Topside Press, 2014.
15. Jules Gill-Peterson, *Histories of the Transgender Child*, Minneapolis, University of Minnesota Press, 2018.
16. John Bellamy Foster, 'Marx's Ecology', *Monthly Review Books*, New York, 2000.
17. McKenzie Wark, *Molecular Red: Theory for the Anthropocene*, Brooklyn, Verso Books, 2015.
18. Jordy Rosenberg, 'Afterword', in Jules Joanne Gleeson and Elle O'Rourke, eds, *Transgender Marxism*, London, Pluto Press, 2021.
19. S J Langer, *Theorizing Transgender Identity for Clinical Practice*, Philadelphia, Jessica Kingsley Publishers, 2019.

Harriet Harriss and Severn Eaton, 2021. Post-apocalyptic visions of the future conceive an architecture in ruins. Here, the 'forest floor' is moribund. However, in the 'Binary-Free Zone', it is alive and fecund – ripe for reproduction.

Non-Binary Ecologies?

Harriet Harriss and Naomi House

'It matters what ideas we use to think other ideas.'
Donna Haraway[1]

Binaries and non-binaries

The title of this article implies that the authors are convinced of three things, none of which are true.

The first is that queer ecology – a nomenclature of ecological philosophy that examines nature and sexuality through the lens of queer theory and non-binary thought – is an ideological proto-parent of non-binary ecologies, when in fact intersexual, trans, pansexual, asexual, genderqueer, lesbian, gay and bi ecologies have yet to be more keenly theorised and may yet possess stronger genetic ties.

The second is that *non-binary ecology* is our propositional thesis and not anti-thesis, when in fact we are uncomfortable with the implied double-duality of binary and non-binary. In general, we find the splicing of theoretical and philosophical terms is often used as a crude way to make a claim, falsely, to new concepts, ideas and even disciplines. A way of illustrating our contention with 'non-binarity' (a term we just invented, in order to prove a point) involves digging a finger into the relationship between dualism, which the humanities defines as 'mind body separation', and its scientific doppelgänger, duality theory; which recognises the 'optimisation efficiencies' that a two-perspective, binary approach can yield, and that the prevailing rich–poor economic segregation of capitalism has made exploitative utility of. Of course, as anyone forced to do mind-numbing physical labour in a warehouse will know, separating the engine of 'optimisation' from its toll on their mind and body is almost impossible. Consequently, what the digging finger of enquiry seeks to do is challenge the false binary between the dualisms and dualities of the humanities and sciences. Not only do their socio-political, self-serving similarities reveal a troubling complicity in relation to the capitalist project, they also bleed through into the epistemologies and disciplines that they have manufactured, and in doing so tune out the binary-defying white noise of the humanities' claim to subjectivity and the sciences' claim to objectivity. Frankly, they are in this together.

And this leads us to what we suspect will be the third misassumption regarding our intentions; that we are necessarily interested in being among the first to assert the conceptual or operational potential or even existence of non-binary ecologies (our academic colleagues cited here will testify to that), or indeed to make any assertion at all. Instead, we are far more keenly interested in the idea of pre-assumption, 'pre-conception', pre-epistemology and potentially even *pre-ecology*, given ecology's structuring and stratifying meaning, and industrial origins and residual associations. Further, we are seeking to 'think ideas' outside of forms of 'established knowledge' that have largely been produced by a small, privileged demographic, and impose a set of obligations with which each subsequent knowledge producer needs to engage. Within academia, knowledge creation is more often valued and rewarded if it appears to build upon the knowledge of this particular demographic; a strategy that we evidently continue to practise in this article, despite our protestations. Criticality offers no immunity, because criticality is still an act of homage. Binarily perhaps, criticality still needs to 'acknowledge knowledge', reinforcing its existence if not also its significance, in doing so. For example, to be 'anti-cat' requires acknowledging that there is a cat to begin with. However, in the case of Schrödinger's cat, the paradox of 'quantum superposition' – the minimum amount of any physical entity involved in an interaction that occurs when two or more quantum properties are

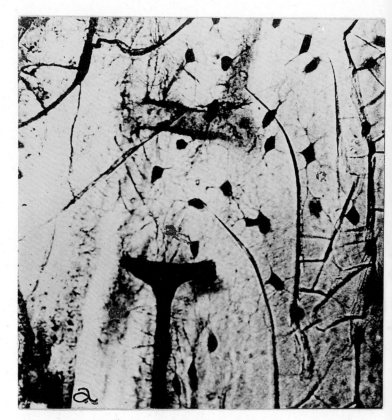

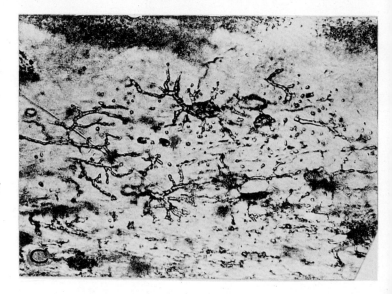

The pre-conceptual architectures of non-binary ecology? Ancient bacteria and fungi: a) colonies of 'cultures' of bacteria are often fossilised, b) mycelia and sporangia, c) scattered bacteria in plant cells, d) other fossil plant cells.

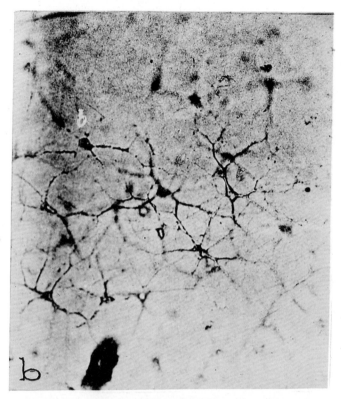

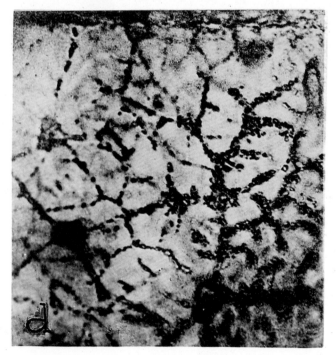

added together, or 'superposed', resulting in another valid quantum state – renders all knowledge hypothetical because in a linear sense, whether the cat is alive or dead inside the box, until we know the outcome, the cat is both alive and dead, or rather alive and non-alive.

However, in a pre-knowledge scenario, we might instead choose to look beyond Schrödinger's academic authority and question whether there is indeed any cat at all. Pre-knowledge (not to be confused with prior knowledge), much like a human infant's lack of self-awareness, does not discern the prescribed binary between the humanities and sciences, or the many boundaries between epistemologies and disciplines in general. If this 'Binary-Free Zone' had an architecture, it would be fluid, damp, soft and sticky and infinitely animated, with a pungent, muggy aroma, not dissimilar to a forest floor, with live cats – and dead ones – whose decaying bones are enmeshed within 'tentacular'[2] underground mycelium networks.

A *non-binary ecology* does not fail to define a person or thing in terms of another; rather it avoids these constructs to begin with. Indeed it avoids any form of identification with existing knowledge frameworks at all. Even the word 'ecology' is binary in that it quite literally means *the branch of science dealing with the relationship of living things to their environments*, as though the two can be separated, or indeed, that ecologies are not comprised of dead things as much as living things, as compost and dead cats readily illustrate. From our perspective, what we are most interested in imagining (but not necessarily proposing or theorising) are the ways in which our thoughts and actions would differ were we entangled by the tentacles of non-binary ecology's pre-conceptual architectures.

Specimen hybridities

To argue that binaries are problematic would be uncharacteristically non-binary of us. But much like 3D goggles, binaries can prove useful accessories with which to see things differently. As with the cat and anti-cat conundrum, Black feminism is an acknowledgement that white feminism exists, whether or not there are white feminists. The main problem with white feminism is not that it failed to achieve gender equality – even with hetero, male–female white privilege in common – but that it refused to look beyond the binary of white male–female power relations for long enough to create the agency so sorely needed by those experiencing racism, classism and other forms of violent, systemic oppression.

Beyond Black feminism and white feminism there are of course many other prefix feminisms, such as liberal, radical, eco, Marxist and beyond, and none of them are necessarily tethered to feminism's historic 'waves', either. There is an implied 'hybridity' to a word like feminism that accommodates so many prefixes and traverses many waves, but this doesn't necessarily make it non-binary. For Nicolas Nova in *A Bestiary of the Anthropocene*, species comprised of two or more animals from different genera are 'specimens' of hybridisation that have largely come into existence since the mid-twentieth century's period of 'Great Acceleration'.[3] These 'specimens' – while historically considered mythical, strange, anomalous, deformed or mutant – defy binary notions of 'cross-contamination' between the 'natural' and the 'artificial',[4] and instead exhibit the variations possible *within* species, not just between them. In the same way that not all *anthropos* (humans) experience the Anthropocene equally, as Black feminism points out, these 'specimens' – with which many of us identify – can operate as intersectional amalgams of hybridisation, offering a new perception of environmental politics. What they also do, through their forms, their actions and their needs – is determine a set of motifs and even emergent spatial typologies that might prefigure a new, Esperanto-style architectural language.

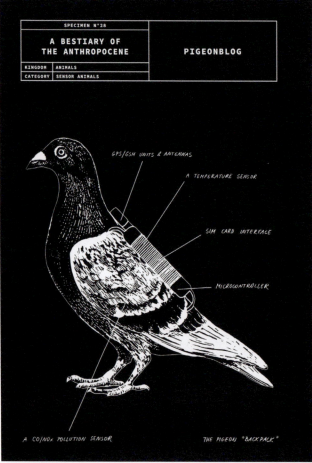

Above: Louis Jean Desprez, depiction of a 'chimera', a hybrid mythological creature, which he turns into a three-headed desert monster hunting for food in front of a rundown palace in North Africa, c.1777–84. The partly digested carcass of its last victim still sticks out of its rib cage and the ground is littered with animal remains.

Below: Nicolas Nova, PigeonBlog, *A Bestiary of the Anthropocene*. Designed by Beatriz da Costa, PigeonBlog is an example of a 'blogject' – an object that blogs – in this case gathering air pollution data and sharing this in real time.[5]

Post futurities

There are multiple layers of binary conceit in the term *post-anthropo-centric*. The term 'anthropo' positions us as the species 'starchitect', assuming exclusive authority without acknowledging the contribution or even the existence of others, that is further reinforced by reference to 'centrism', a political theory that insists that social justice and social hierarchy can be achieved simultaneously. The added flourish of 'post-' asserts that we are fundamentally past our systems of self-privileging, when it is starkly obvious that we are not. 'Post' posturing exposes some of the tedium associated with the growing body of ecological discourse situated within 'futurity', a term which has come to mean the quality of being or happening in the future, without actually knowing what the future is. For us, there is a despondent quality to futurity, which can manifest as atrophying 'climate grief' or an abandonment of action in anticipation of a techno-utopian climate 'solution', deployed against miscreant asteroids, and badly designed planets. Strangely, but not unrelatedly, 'futurity' also means a horse race, typically for two-year-old geldings, in which the competitors are nominated at birth or before.[6] Futurity is about as much a claim to territory as an American flag on the Moon, and as reliable as a prenuptial agreement. Futurity presupposes that we have a stake in the future – or is it post-future? – that evokes the vain assumption of 'post-anthropocentrism' that we will survive into the future at all. All futures have already been determined, in terms of planetary prognosis. There is little agency left, and what exists, if history is able to supply reliable data sets – may permit some of the anthro-perpetrators the chance to offer some form of amelioration for a handful of species, but not necessarily our own.

Mycelium networks – a Binary-Free Zone that is fluid, damp, soft and sticky and infinitely animated.

Ruinous precarity

The Anthropcene's 'condition of precarity' connects the Amazon warehouse to the Amazon basin. From a popular culture perspective, however, anthropocentric precarity is routinely misrepresented as one universally catastrophic event, rather than an incremental, quotidian, multi-species death-march that has been underway for several decades. More often, apocalyptic imagery, while strangely compelling if not also numbing, shows symptoms of advanced-stage anthropocenic narcissism, whereby the perpetrators are lionised and wrongly exonerated through depictions of 'heroicisms' in the face of nature's alleged wrath. While the urgency of our current climate crisis predicament might not have been authored collectively, and nor is it felt collectively, it can only be fixed collectively. As 'individuals' – by this we mean individual identities, abilities, regions, nations – we have no hope of survival, and it is this collectivity that demands we hybridise into 'all terrain critters',[7] departitioning our sense of selves from those of other species. By defying binaries and manifesting hybridity, critters use collectivism as a catalyst for evolving new forms of 'care' in response to the precarious conditions of the Anthropocene. Like matsutake mushrooms, they 'survive collaboratively in disturbance and contamination',[8] amid the ruins of late-stage capitalism. What especially intrigues us about matsutake mushrooms is their status as mycorrhiza; a type of species that is symbiotically both a fungus and a plant. Not only do they grow underneath forest floor 'litter' but their pungent aroma is reported as 'unpleasant',[9] despite their status as a 'delicacy'. While some readers might find the idea of a 'litter'-eating future closely evocative of the apocalyptic imagery that we contested earlier, urban farms, food-producing community gardens and what British readers would understand as 'allotments' evidence that we are already familiar with small-scale prototypes that typically appeared on abandoned and neglected city sites in response to collective need. In the British example, planting allotments on bomb-sites was even actively encouraged by the then government in order to address food shortages. Mycorrhizally emerging from the 'litter' of ruined cities, this was one manifestation of adaptive precarity – the dualities and dualisms between what constitutes food production and food waste resituated within the Binary-Free Zone.

Moss growing on rocks. 'We're busy looking for biological, ecological and cultural solutions to climate chaos,' says Kimmerer. 'But mosses, which have been with us ever since they arose, 400 million years ago, have endured every climate change that has ever happened.'[10]

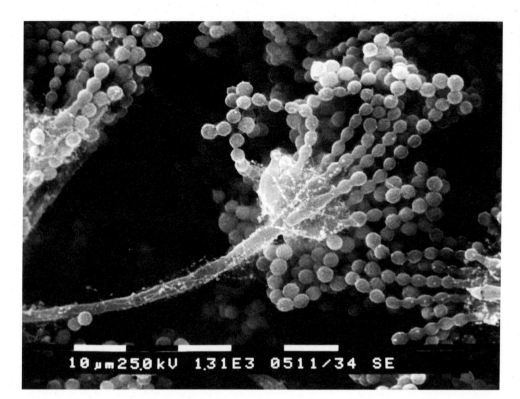

Aspergillus fumigatus is a species of fungus that is thought to reproduce asexually. Asexual reproduction problematises our conditioned understanding of gender binaries.

'Litter' collectivisms

Much like the scavenging, unregulated, litter-foraging collectivism of wartime and postwar London, mosses are similarly expert in adjusting to their immediate surroundings using ludic strategies. Mosses have persisted across geological ages, finding ways to survive even in the face of climate crisis, and are the ultimate adaptable species, thriving in adversity and ruination.[11] As with mycelia, mosses resilience discreetly extrapolates authentic anthropocenic scenarios, by providing the prototypes needed for us to imagine what collaborative relationships, infrastructures for inter-species interactions, collectivisms of care and litter consumption could actually look like. Their ability to have survived all five of the previous mass extinctions connects us to a sense of pre-knowing that has otherwise become clouded with capitalism-serving narratives determined to distract us from an accurate rendering of the already-underway anthropocentric apocalypse, and the possibility of a collective existence that could mitigate it. Species-aggrandising 'cli-fi'[12] depictions of white men shooting Earth-destroying asteroids from space, or threatening to deploy architecture as a weapon of refurbishment and reprimand against a badly designed planet,[13] fail to recognise that mycelia and mosses run a system approach whose sophistication far exceeds any that the anthropos species has yet proven capable of. This is not to suggest that (poorer, hungry) anthropos should mimic mosses, eat rubbish and stop complaining about the precarious conditions in which they find themselves, but that the possibility of a future relies upon models of collective existence that situate us all among the 'litter'.

To do this requires us to assume a degree of species humility with which we are almost entirely unfamiliar. Capitalism's enduring success and continuing dominance proves unequivocally that our 'systems thinking' is profoundly inferior in comparison to that of other species. Our systems – easily boiled down into a tussle between the binarity of left and right (politics) – have earned us the lonely accolade of becoming the world's pre-eminent serial killers, not only of all other species but also our own. It therefore seems reasonable to suppose that anyone attempting to identify alternatives to self-annihilation needs to look beyond species-specific histories and to 400-million-year-old mosses in order to understand how these 'rootless', resilient plants that are quick to reinhabit disturbed or destroyed landscapes bring (soil) stability and end food scarcity (by absorbing and sharing moisture), and in doing so, exhibit aspects of litter collectivism that indiscriminately sustains and cares for all life forms.[14]

Nature, nurture, naurture

Of course, acts of litter collectivism extend far beyond sharing food. Sexual sustenance involves interactions that serve multiple needs beyond the pursuit of reproduction-as-metric-driven Darwinism. Although non-binarity is situated as 'queer' rather than 'heterosexual', nature has long been weaponised against the queer community, in an attempt to dislocate queerness from nature, or, from its natural self.[15] The binary of nature/nurture is entirely debunked by the fact that there are over 1,500 species besides humans that engage in 'acts of homosexuality' – that we know of, and importantly, that some scientists are necessarily willing to admit to.[16] Homosexual activity is not only common but also essential. In the case of the dwarf chimpanzee – an entirely bisexual species and one of our closest relatives – 'sex plays a conspicuous role in all activities and takes the focus away from violence, which is the most typical method of solving conflicts among primates and many other animals'.[17] Even mosses have variable sexual systems, with the ability to produce male, female and hermaphrodite plants, which recent research suggests is the evolutionary result of interspecies sex.[18] Indeed, it is the polyamorous fluidity of sexual interactions within the Binary-Free Zone that serves to destabilise the binaries between nature and nurture, 'queering' them in the process. Notional 'differences' between genders, identities, sexualities and species engage a form of *intramolecular* transition much like a 'constantly mutating socius'.[19] In this fluid state, the binary of nature and nurture is superseded by *naurture hybridisms*, composite live forms capable of radically altering the environment in which they are situated through their own transformation.

The IQE's 'Habitat 1: Regenerative Interactive Zone of Nurture' simulates a 'safe space' within which everyone and everything has agency. Using 'participatory artwork' that takes the form of a social simulation game, queerness is retrieved from the margins as 'the warm illumination of a horizon imbued with potentiality ... an ideality that can be distilled from the past and used to imagine a future'. Commissioned by the Guggenheim Museum as part of the exhibition Countryside, The Future (February 2020 – February 2021).[20]

Unendings

From the atom bomb to the plastic straw, the dairy industry to the disposable razor, anthropos have long used objects to take the blame for all kinds of climate crimes, dissociating themselves from the 'things' that are fleetingly new and relevant, that soon become old and obsolete. This waste in transit is the very foodstuff of ownership, property and entitlement that characterises capitalism's precarity. Confronting the distinctions that segregate 'everything' from 'everyone', or, 'things' from 'ones' is the last of our antagonisms with binarity. The problem rests with object-oriented ontology[21] or 'triple O', a twenty-first-century, Heideggerian school of thought that rejects the privileging of human existence over the existence of non-human objects, implying an object autonomy not dissimilar to our own. This hyperbole has, without irony, advanced the notion of 'hyperobjects', to refer to objects that operate on a scale so vast and that are so massively distributed in time and space as to transcend 'spatiotemporal specificity'.[22]

From our perspective, hyperobjects do in fact possess 'spatiotemporal specificity' – for example – when the 200 million middle-class, mostly caucasian SUV drivers[23] are 'spatially and temporally and specifically' forcing 1.5 billion mostly black and brown people to flee their homes (many on foot) as a direct consequence of the contribution to global heating that their choice of vehicle enacts.[24] All too easily, *hyperobjectivity* fails to acknowledge that climate dissociation is not only ecologically destructive, but profoundly racist – in destabilising human/object hierarchies, it masks an unavoidable truth – that objects articulate and manifest our intentions precisely. There is no binary between climate justice and social justice. The two can only be achieved simultaneously.

Upendings

There is no such thing as a disposable object. The infinitute of anthropic object-waste is overwhelming a planet of almost 8 billion people who produce almost 2.3 billion tons of it per day.[25] Despite an end to colonial rule by OECD[26] countries, residual imperialist infrastructures have continued to exploit the assets and diminish the wealth of the Global South, which continues to operate as the dustbin for its waste and pollution. More recently however, an increasing number of these countries from the Global South are banning plastic waste imports, and even sending back the billions of tons of object-waste they previously accommodated.[27] This object-waste displacement brings a more authentic, albeit dystopian, reading of the term 'recycling' as this tsunami of denial pulls a U-turn and comes right back at us. As the example of Trash Island – a 700,000 km^2 conglomeration of waste and murdered aquatic life the size of Russia, that is currently volleying between Hawaii and California in the Pacific Ocean[28] – serves to illustrate, masses of waste-objects are not only destructive, they are cannibalistic too, growing in scale, turning lives into carcasses and attracting more of its own malevolent materiality.

More deadly, however, is the 'hyperobject' version of this bloated and burgeoning mass that manifests at the scale of the nano-particle. These invisible, airborne and waterborne hyper-waste-objects – encompassing pesticide residues and traffic pollution, NOx gases and (agriculturally produced) oestrogen in drinking water[29] – are barely discernible by contemporary pollution- and contaminant-measuring systems, and easily enter lungs and bloodstreams. In doing so, and perhaps as *the ultimate act of non-binarity*, anthropos are no longer separated from hyper-waste-objects, but have *become* hyper-waste-objects. We are the asteroid at the scale of Trash Island, we are the stardust at the scale of the toxic nano-particle. We are in our spacesuits shooting at the asteroids inside of ourselves. We are staring at our nano-particle selves in an infinity mirror. Like the mosses and fungi in the Binary-Free Zone, the only possible hope is to be entirely upended – thrown in with the litter and other critters, mycorrhizally departitioned, bat-blind and earth-worm-inarticulate (lest we default to our usual excuses) but endowed with hypersensitive ears that connect us to the reverberations, throbbing, ripping, scratching and bubbling sounds that are discernible only when we listen.

Opposite: *Severn Eaton*, Stardust Bath Collective, acrylic on wood panel, 2010. To paraphrase Joni Mitchell, the 'stardust' we are comprised of is a deadly amalgamation of 'billion-year-old carbon' hyper-waste-objects whose only hope is to return to the 'garden' – or, more precisely, the Binary Free Zone.

1. Donna Haraway, *Staying with the Trouble: Making Kin in the Chthulucene*, Durham, NC, Duke University Press, 2016. p103.
2. Donna Haraway uses the phrase 'tentacular thinking' in *Staying with the Trouble* (2016, p32), referencing tentacular animals and plants such as spiders and fungi that represent 'life lived along lines'. She expands the definition of 'tentacular' outwards to further embrace IT networks and the 'cloud'.
3. The term the 'Great Acceleration' is a phrase that captures the period post-1950, in which human-related activities have resulted in rapid change.
4. Nicolas Nova and Disinovation.Org, *A Bestiary of the Anthropocene: On Hybrid Minerals, Animals, Plants, Fungi*, Eindhoven, Onomatopee, 2021, p7.
5. Nicolas Nova and Disinovation.Org, *A Bestiary of the Anthropocene: On Hybrid Minerals, Animals, Plants, Fungi*, Eindhoven, Onomatopee, 2021, p79.
6. A 'futurity' is a horse competition or race usually for younger horses, where nominations are made well in advance, sometimes even prior to the horse's birth.
7. Donna Haraway is referencing Anna Tsing, p37.
8. Anna Lowenhaupt Tsing, cited in Haraway (2016, p37). Extending Anna's thesis beyond mushrooms, Warren Cornwall offers an illustration of Tsing's thesis in action in an article discussing the collaboration of human engineering and coral reefs.
9. Source: https://en.wikipedia.org/wiki/Matsutake.
10. Rachel Cooke, 'Robin Wall Kimmerer: 'Mosses are a model of how we might live'', *The Guardian*, 19 June 2021, https://www.theguardian.com/science/2021/jun/19/robin-wall-kimmerer-gathering-moss-climate-crisis-interview?CMP=Share_iOSApp_Other.
11. Darwin's Paradox questions how some life forms such as coral reefs – and in this case mosses – are able to survive in hostile conditions. Coral reefs utilise sponges that absorb nutrients and redistribute them across its ecosystem. See 'Darwin's Paradox', Shape of Life, https://www.shapeoflife.org/news/general-news/2020/09/21/darwin%E2%80%99s-paradox.
12. Meaning 'climate science-fiction' – a subgenre of science-fiction or sci-fi literature or film – that deals with a broad array of climate crisis themes.
13. In October 2020, BIG Architects founder Bjarke Ingels announced he was drawing up a masterplan for the Earth to 'prove that a sustainable human presence on planet Earth is attainable with existing technologies', provoking much derision in response to the imperialist and even sexist overtones of his statement. Source: India Block, 'Masterplanet is Bjarke Ingels' plan to redesign Earth and stop climate change', *Dezeen*, 27 October 2020, https://www.dezeen.com/2020/10/27/bjarke-ingels-big-masterplanet-climate-change-architecture-news/.
14. 'Inter-species sex is behind the gender gradient in mosses', *The BioPhiles* (blog), 12 June 2015, https://biophilesblog.wordpress.com/2015/06/12/interspecies-sex-is-behind-the-gender-gradient-in-mosses/; see also: Tim Radford, 'All hail the humble moss, bringer of oxygen and life to Earth', *The Guardian*, 15 August 2016, https://www.theguardian.com/science/2016/aug/15/all-hail-the-humble-moss-bringer-of-oxygen-and-life-to-earth.
15. Within Nicole Seymour's book, *Strange Natures: Futurity, Empathy, and the Queer Ecological Imagination*, Jeffrey Weeks proposes that queer history provides a lens through which we can discern whether what we assume to be natural is in fact social. Nicole Seymour, *Strange Natures, Futurity, Empathy, and the Queer Ecological Imagination*, Chicago, University of Illinois Press, 2013, p91.
16. This was the thesis underpinning the 'Against Nature's Order?' exhibition at the Oslo Natural History Museum in 2006. Petter Boeckman was the academic advisor for the exhibition. Source: '1500 animal species practice homosexuality', *News Medical Life Sciences*, 23 October 2006, https://www.news-medical.net/news/2006/10/23/1500-animal-species-practice-homosexuality.aspx.
17. Ibid.
18. 'Interspecies sex', The BioPhiles.
19. The materiality of this state of connected knowing echoes with Félix Guittari envisioning of 'a nascent subjectivity – a constantly mutating socius – an environment in the process of being reinvented'. Félix Guittari, *The Three Ecologies*, London and New Brunswick, The Athlone Press, 2000, p68.
20. H.O.R.I.Z.O.N. (Habitat 1: Regenerative Interactive Zone of Nurture) was commissioned by the Guggenheim Museum as part of the public programming for the exhibition Countryside, The Future (February 2020 – February 2021), https://queerecology.org/H-O-R-I-Z-O-N.
21. OOO or triple O stands for object-oriented ontology – a branch of philosophy that perceives the 'vitality in even non-living matter' – Landon Schnabel, 'The question of subjectivity in three emerging feminist science studies frameworks: Feminist postcolonial science studies, new feminist materialisms, and queer ecologies', *Women's Studies International Forum*, vol. 44, May–June 2014, p2, https://www.sciencedirect.com/science/article/pii/S027753951400034X?via%3Dihub.
22. 'Hypermutable' (p128), 'hyper lucid' (p106) beings were first proposed by philosopher and social theorist Brian Massumi, in *Parables for the Virtual*, Durham, NC, Duke University Press, 2002, then later transposed and expanded by Timothy Morton in *The Ecological Thought*, Cambridge, MA, Harvard University Press, 2010, p130.
23. Ben Webster, 'Soaring demand for SUVs exacerbates climate crisis', *The Times*, 14 November 2019, https://www.thetimes.co.uk/article/soaring-demand-for-suvs-exacerbates-climate-crisis-kbpj5mpzg.
24. The Ecosystem Threat Register anticipates that 1.2 billion people will be displaced by the climate crisis by 2050, although many consider this a conservative estimate. World Economic Forum, https://www.weforum.org/agenda/2021/06/climate-refugees-the-world-s-forgotten-victims.
25. Based upon World Bank indicators, https://datatopics.worldbank.org/world-development-indicators.
26. Organisation for Economic Co-operation and Development.
27. As an example, a Chinese embargo on plastic imports threatens to displace 111 million metric tons of plastic object-waste by 2030. 'Time to stop dumping plastic waste on the Global South', Friends of the Earth Europe, 30 April 2019, https://friendsoftheearth.eu/news/time-to-stop-dumping-plastic-waste-on-the-global-south.
28. Also known as the Great Pacific Garbage Patch (GPGP), Trash Island is the largest of the five offshore plastic accumulation zones in the world's oceans.
29. Tim Smedley, 'The toxic killers in our air too small to see', BBC Future, 15 November 2019, https://www.bbc.com/future/article/20191113-the-toxic-killers-in-our-air-too-small-to-see. Separately, women's contraceptive pills were blamed for oestrogen in drinking water, when in fact most of it comes from animal agriculture.

Non-Binary Ecologies?

Loser Images

A Feminist Proposal for Post-Anthropocene Visuality

Joanna Zylinska

Opposite: *The Blue Marble*, taken during the Voyager 17 mission, 1972.

Below: *Earthrise* (rotated), taken during the Apollo 8 mission, 1968.

Popularised by the *Whole Earth* catalogue, both images played a significant role in raising environmental awareness in the early 1970s, providing an image of our planet as a palpable object that requires our care and attention.

#WhatPlanet?

What planet are you on? Or, as Twitter has it, #WhatPlanet? Usually meant as a challenge, the question probes the epistemological problem of being able (or, indeed, unable) to see and know what one is talking about, to see and feel the ground on which one stands – as well as all the other territories to which this ground is connected. In the context of the unfolding Anthropocene sensibility, this question has been used by broadcast media – from the BBC to RTÉ – more literally, as a way of urging the public to pay attention to environmental and climate issues.[1] Given that attention is not just conceptual but also, or maybe even primarily, visual, we need to heed art historian John Tresch's argument that 'how we live on earth is closely tied to how we address the immensely difficult task of picturing the universe'.[2] In our efforts to understand, manage and counter the Anthropocene, it is therefore important to question how we see our planet – i.e., how it arrives to us as *an image*, and how specific images of planetarity shape our imagination and ideas.

So how *can* we observe the diverse conditions, multiple architectures and ongoing transformations of Planet Earth? How can we envisage a different model of our habitat? What vantage point should we adopt in the process? The 2019 issue of *Architectural Design* edited by Liam Young and outlining the notion of 'architectures of the post-Anthropocene' is one attempt to approach this problem. Illustrated with elegantly crisp photographs of 'architecture without people', it demonstrates the recent emergence of 'landscapes made for or by machines',[3] featuring data centres, giant distribution warehouses, telecommunications infrastructures and industrialised agriculture lots. Many of the images in that special issue had been created with the help of drone camera technology, flattened perspective and CGI, resulting in an oddly detached picture of the world. Even if this new world looks distinctly post-human, the all-conquering visual apparatus used to conjure it has ended up elevating Man as the creator and destroyer of worlds. As a feminist rejoinder to such an antiseptic aesthetic of the post-Anthropocene, in this article I propose a concept of 'loser images'. Offered, with a nod to artist–writer Hito Steyerl, in defence of the poor image of the Earth,[4] this concept has been developed from two planetary case studies (including one from my own art practice) as a way of imagining a different vision of, and a different relationship to, our habitat.

Joanna Zylinska, *Planetary Exhalation*, 2021. Composite image with a beach ball photographed on carpeted surface, produced as part of a critical–practical investigation into ways of imaging our planet in the Anthropocene – and of imagining better ways of living *on* it.

#amazingdroneposts

Many of the theorists engaging with planetary thinking today do so in dialogue with post-colonial writer Gayatri Chakravorty Spivak's essay 'Planetarity' from her short book *Death of a Discipline*, published in 2002. Writing about the transformation of literary studies into a global discipline, Spivak opposes the abstraction of globalisation, which she sees as 'the imposition of the same system of exchange everywhere',[5] to the differentiated political space of planetarity. 'The planet is in the species of alterity, belonging to another system; and yet we inhabit it, on loan,' she writes.[6] For her, the planetary perspective is always partial. It is also a demand and a call to responsibility. Building on Spivak's argument, I want to suggest that if we are to enact the ethico-political injunction of her original idea, we need *better conceptualisations and better images* of our planet.

Daily image practices performed in online spaces constitute a labour-intensive laboratory for creating perceptions of Planet Earth – and of ourselves as its inhabitants. This brings me to my first case study: the widely popular photographs of different parts of our globe taken by amateur and semi-professional drone operators, and presented on social media. I am particularly intrigued by the flow of conventionally beautiful stills (and occasional short videos) of various picturesque locations and impressive buildings – New Zealand's Mount Taranaki, coastal ice formations somewhere in Canada, Dubai's night-lit cityscape – posted on Instagram under the hashtag #amazingdroneposts. No matter whether they feature natural land formations or human-made artefacts, the drone gaze those images espouse is determinedly architectural. Avoiding any pretence at naturalism, they present the world as a time- and labour-led formation, even if the temporal scales of the labourer are not always human. The machine eye of the drone camera (mostly belonging to one of the Mavic or Mini drones from the industry leader DJI) is deployed to see *for us* humans – but also, of course, to see *better than* us.

The hyperrealist imagery deploys high contrast and geometrical lines. These images are easy to see and be amazed by, because they inscribe themselves in the schematism of human perception outlined by psychologist James Gibson, serving the world to us as a 'layout of surfaces',[7] and not a sequence of three-dimensional Cartesian coordinates. According to Gibson, humans have no depth perception. What we see are edges, layouts and surfaces, with the image gradually emerging as an image through our movement in the

Screenshot of the #amazingdroneposts Instagram feed, 8 March 2021. It is an automatic compilation of posts by different users, featuring drone images of various 'amazing' locations from around the globe.

Loser Images: A Feminist Proposal for Post-Anthropocene Visuality world. Gibson's ecological theory of visual perception offers a dynamic account of not only how we see the world but also of how the world *becomes something* to us. If the purpose of vision 'is to be aware of the surroundings, the ambient environment',[8] perception involves information pick-up from the world, but it also involves gathering information about ourselves by *moving through* the world – and, in the process, sensing ourselves as different from it. In Gibson's framework, vision is thus both self-forming and terraforming.

How does this model of vision help us see and understand the Instagram feed of #amazingdroneposts? The images posted under this hashtag represent the world reduced to surfaces. To say this is not to castigate those images for their superficiality or banality – although there *is* a visual sameness to the #amazingdroneposts image feed, with the relatively narrow set of aesthetic and technical criteria for what this amazingness represents. However, they are surfaces the way *all* technical images are, as understood by philosopher Vilém Flusser. Technical images, be they photographs or video, for Flusser represent a two-dimensional flattening of the world; a transformation of its linearity into code.[9] The schematism of those drone posts results in images that look more like graphs than photographs. They thus end up serving as visualisations of the world and not its representations. There is a subgenre to those images which includes humans as insignificant moving points, performing superhuman feats such as jogging at the edge of a cliff or scaling a vertical rock. Some of those scenes are cut through with close-up machine-eye shots from GoPro Hero action cameras, worn on bodies. No matter whether humans are included in those pictures or not, there is heroism implied in all of them, with the masterful eye of the drone performing amazing acts. The images are sometimes accompanied by heroic narratives of the (predominantly invisible) operator almost losing the drone, and then having to scale icebergs and plunge into volcanoes to rescue it.

The #amazingdroneviews images are easy to take in: they afford the world to us as both a surface and an uninterrupted flow. And yet, because they are to be consumed by largely immobile human bodies placed in front of screens, with movement limited to the eye scan and finger scroll, they outsource the action of terraforming mobility to the drone machine. Gibson predicted this experience when he wrote, nearly three decades ago, that 'We modern, civilized, indoor adults are so accustomed to looking at a page or a picture, or through a window, that we often lose the feeling of being surrounded by the environment, our sense of the ambient array of light … We live boxed up lives.'[10] In the era of pandemic-induced lockdowns, working from home and Zoom education this experience has been expanded to the almost universal form of epistemological encounter with images – and with people reduced to images. This semi-immersive experience creates a sense of easy and total accessibility; an illusion of the world being there on demand, subject to our gaze and capital's desire. In this way, it becomes a model of globalisation, articulated by Spivak as 'the imposition of the same system of exchange everywhere'.

Feminist with a drone
In an attempt to identify technical and conceptual openings within the dominant structures of planetary visibility, I have developed an art project called Feminist with a Drone, which serves here as my second case study. The (mock-ethnographic) 'field notes' presented below, and the accompanying images, are part of this artwork. But Feminist with a Drone is not just an artwork but also a *thinkwork*: it is an attempt to outline ideas and concepts *with practices and things*.

Below and opposite: Joanna Zylinska, from *Loser Images 1.0* (Feminist with a Drone), 2021. Photographs taken with a toy drone.

On 12 December 2020 I purchased a Ryze Tello drone. Designed by industry giant DJI, this mini drone, marketed as 'the most fun drone ever', is aimed at teaching kids and adults 'how awesome flying can be'. The exploration of this awesomeness was the key goal of my fieldwork. My first outing with the Tello took place on 24 December 2020, in a small park in a residential area of southwest London. During the flight times of up to 13 minutes, I captured a sequence of still and moving images from a height of 2–10 metres. The experiment came to a halt when the drone flew away on descent. The follow-up search didn't yield any results, the situation compounded by unpropitious weather conditions and approaching dusk, with the drone then considered lost. The following day the drone was located in a different part of the park. The experiment in testing the drone's awesomeness was resumed the following week. Some images were taken during the first flight. On its second ascent the drone lost one of its propellers, with the propeller itself becoming lost among the park's vegetation. A replacement propeller was installed, but this made the drone inoperative, with the device losing the capacity to fully lift off the ground. This concluded my attempt to fly the drone and take images with it. Loss was a key characteristic of my experience with the Ryze Tello.

The Hypothesis and questions about the observation
Could things have gone any worse? Was the fieldwork conducted as part of my project a failure? Crucially, should I have bought a better, more 'manly' and more high-tech drone? In the spirit of feminist bricolage, an approach which remains aware of power relations, while foregrounding 'the practices of shaping, crafting, and producing that academics usually hide (and often hide behind) in the production of beautiful and polished surfaces, unpunctured by doubts, hesitations and incompletion',[11] I decided to repurpose my losses. The limited sample of images obtained from the drone's camera and their relatively low quality, coupled with the loss of the drone's functionality, led to the development of a hypothesis about the possibility of constructing an alternative drone visuality, which I termed 'loser images'.

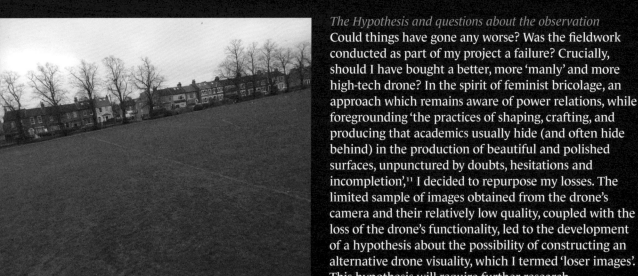

As a feminist rejoinder to the 'amazing' drone views discussed in my first case study, I am offering 'loser images' as a figuration that channels some of the potential of the multi-perspectival, humachinic worldview without falling for its grandeur of scale. Figurations, used in the work of feminist thinkers of technology such as Donna Haraway or Rosi Braidotti, are thought devices aimed at 'shaping a different political imaginary or performing an alternative image of the future'.[12] Yet rather than propose a straightforward return to a more human or humane perspective in response to this master vision of 'architecture without people', I want to probe further the creative potential of decoupling sight from a bipedal human body and dispersing it across the environment. I am thus interested in mobilising the same image-making technology to enact a less masterful, less heroic and less domineering way of visioning and imaging. This alternative form of post-Anthropocene visuality does not flatten the world into a postcard while excising its inhabitants of different scales from the picture. Instead, it envisages a more porous *planetscape* – and a more entangled and messy ecology.

Loser images for a planetary micro-vision
The notion of 'loser images' embraces the loss of the anchoring of vision in the bipedal human body and its dispersal across the environment. But it also loses the heroism of the humachinic gaze perpetuated by the dominant drone visuality. My minor intervention into the grand problem of planetarity has an affinity with Heather McLean's 'praise of chaotic research pathways'.[13] McLean points out that there is something both totalising and limiting about the planetary approach many theorists offer, in that it 'privileges a lineage of particular white, male, and European Marxist and neo-Marxist political economists at the expense of feminist, queer, and anti-colonial contributions to this sub-field'.[14]

It also positions researchers as pre-constituted and monadic entities, not as living breathing beings emerging as part of their work, praxis or struggle.

My 'loser images' go beyond the perfect planetary vision of the drone eye – but they also transcend the airy planetarity of much of contemporary architecture and urban theory, which seems to have left behind Spivak's commitment to partial views, inhabitation and an alterity that makes a difference. Conceptually, Feminist with a Drone engages humour, irony and partiality as feminist companion methods for conducting work in technoscience and technoculture. Those modes of affectively remodulating the traditional framework of what counts as knowledge and scholarship open up alternative ways of seeing and doing. McLean also works in this vein – for example, with her drag-king performance at a cabaret called Fail Better, a Glasgow space featuring artists of colour, and queer and working-class artists. Yet she admits that such activities could be positioned as ineffective and fears that local sites of activism may end up looking 'weak and useless in the face of steamroller-like neoliberal policies'.[15] I share McLean's concerns; yet, like her, I believe there is too much at stake to just give up. Feminist with a Drone was thus designed as a performance of *planetarity as a research problem*, but it also was already a form of *research designed as a performance*. My goal with this was to perform the study of planetarity, and of the associated disciplines of art history, ethnography, geography, urban studies, architecture and design, differently. Even though the method and the tools used (a toy drone, a beach ball in the parallel project called Planetary Expiration, p34) may seem naïve and childlike, their underlying ambition – to challenge our ongoing planetary foolishness as well as our partial vision – is very serious indeed.

The 'loser images' figuration produced in the process follows in the footsteps of Hito Steyerl, whose kin notion of 'poor images' has become an important

Joanna Zylinska, from *Loser Images 2.0 (Same Energy)*, 2021. Composite image, made with the Same Energy visual search engine, in response to the author's photograph taken with a toy drone.

Joanna Zylinska, from *Loser Images 2.0 (Same Energy)*, 2021. Composite image, made with the Same Energy visual search engine, in response to the author's photograph of a beach ball.

trope in contemporary critical studies of the image. Steyerl proposed the term to refer to lossy digital images traversing the networked personal computers of our globe. Their poverty referred to their low quality and low resolution as a result of their incessant replication on ever cheaper media, but it also pointed to the wider condition of cultural disjuncture, where the impoverishment of many image producers and imaged subjects went hand in hand with the enrichment of those in control of digital infrastructures. My 'loser images' are precisely such *poor images of the world*: serving as counterpoints to the #amazingdroneviews of Planet Earth, they are a testament to the poor quality of the camera and the limited skills of its operator. There is something not quite right with them as both representations and captures. The worldview they present is out of sync: wobbly, smeary, somehow degraded. Yet these 'loser images' are not just mine: with the concept, enacted here not only through my project but also, thanks to the deep-learning similarity algorithm of the visual search engine Same Energy (which is similar to Google's search by image, but more look- and mood-based), they inaugurate an open-ended archive from which a different picture of the planet can emerge.[16]

Picking up the baton from Steyerl, I am thus speaking here in defence of the poor image of the world: low resolution, widely accessible, pirated. In other words, I am speaking for what we might term, with a nod to Gary Hall, an ethical piracy. In *Pirate Philosophy*, Hall revisits the Latin origins of the verb *pirao*, which meant to 'make an attempt, try, test … endeavour, attack',[17] to refer to piratic practices in texts and images which go against the grain of traditional knowledge production, its classification and distribution. Loser images are pirate images because they 'tease [and] give trouble',[18] as per the word's Greek etymology. Loser images also drop out of the competitive system of accolades, prizes and totems. They drop out of individual authorship. Their marginal cultural status is not by itself a guarantee of progressivism: we know the right can meme too!

To speak in defence of the poor image of the world is to mobilise an ethical injunction to see the world better – and to make better things in it. It is an injunction to look around and askew, to look obliquely, to work against the limitations of the image, and to know that the picture is always partial. 'Loser images' also challenge the heroism of the drone eye and the GoPro Hero camera. Offering a fragile yet tender look, they differ from 'ruin porn', that is the aestheticisation of loss, decay and poverty which is part of the dominant Anthropocene visuality. There is something not quite right with them, but they are not entirely wrong either. A post-Anthropocene loser image: it is what it is. But it tries to fail better, every time.

1   *What Planet Are We On?*, podcast, BBC Radio 5, broadcast 2020 – ongoing; *What Planet Are You On?*, television programme, RTÉ, broadcast 2019–20.
2   John Tresch, 'Cosmic terrains (of the sun king, son of heaven, and sovereign of the seas)', *e-flux*, no. 114, https://www.e-flux.com/journal, December 2020.
3   Liam Young, ed., *Machine Landscapes: Architectures of the Post Anthropocene*, special issue of *Architectural Design*, no. 257, January–February 2019.
4   Hito Steyerl, 'In defense of the poor image', *e-flux*, no. 10, https://www.e-flux.com/journal, November 2009.
5   Gayatri Chakravorty Spivak, 'Planetarity', in *Death of a Discipline*, New York, Columbia University Press, 2003, p72.
6   Ibid.
7   James Gibson, *The Ecological Approach to Visual Perception*, Boston, Houghton Mifflin, 1979, p148.
8   Ibid., p112.
9   Vilém Flusser, *Into the Universe of Technical Images*, Minneapolis, University of Minnesota Press, 2011.
10 Gibson, *The Ecological Approach to Visual Perception*, p203.
11 Rachel Handforth and Carol A Taylor, 'Doing academic writing differently: A feminist bricolage', *Gender and Education*, vol. 28, no. 5, 2016, pp627–43, p629.
12 Sarah Kember and Joanna Zylinska, 'Media always and everywhere: A cosmic approach', in U Ekman, et al., eds, *Ubiquitous Computing, Complexity and Culture*, New York, Routledge, 2016, pp226–36, p225.
13 Heather McLean, 'In praise of chaotic research pathways: A feminist response to planetary urbanization', *Environment and Planning D: Society and Space*, vol. 36, no. 3, 2018, pp547–55, p547.
14 Ibid., p548.
15 Ibid., p6.
16 Same Engine indexes 19 million images from Reddit, Instagram and Pinterest. See https://same.energy.
17 Gary Hall, Pirate Philosophy: For a Digital Post-humanities, Cambridge, MA, MIT Press, 2016, p140.
18 Ibid.

Planetary Portals in the Upside-Down World

**Casper Laing Ebbensgaard,
Kerry Holden and Kathryn Yusoff**

Michael Salu, Ever in Abeokuta. Red Earth Project, 2020.

Cities, and the architectural emblems we associate with their horizontal advance across the face of the Earth and their vertical expansion into the atmosphere, rely upon the technologies that for more than a century have been reaching further below them. The idea of the skyscraper as an 'inverted mine'[1] conjures images of cross-sections of the Earth where whatever 'goes up' can be mirror-massed in a network of subterranean voids – no volume comes from nowhere; it always has a material and social debt to pay and always casts a shadow, no matter how far away. If, as Gavin Bridge suggests, holes in the Earth not only produce distinct spaces of extraction and accumulation (mines, pits, collieries and so on) but present the 'conduits' or 'points of access' to the layered depths of compressed time (minerals, coals, oils, gases and so on),[2] we might think of skyscrapers and tall structures as the portals into different worlds and dimensions. Buried sunshine[3] begets urban behemoths. Not only do skyscrapers bruise the clouds with their upward thrust and outward projection, but they initiate and mobilise new material states that disperse geochemical flows and alluvial sedimentations across the globe. Under racial capitalism's regulation of capital by race, this pulling up and pushing down of material states requires a parallel subjugation that creates stratas of black and brown (i.e. racialised) under/grounds that uphold the floating city.

In a recent article in *Nature*,[4] scientists claim we have passed a crucial tipping-point as the total mass of human-made matter for the first time outweighs the total biomass of the Earth. While such calculative logics of biomass and anthropogenic forms have a substantive bleed at the interface of ecological entanglements and geological flows, the neat planetary inversion captures the vertical exchanges of the planetary, as the real states and stakes of being planetary. Shifting stuff is not just a concern of political geography but changes states of matter. A change of state is less a territorial proposition of land than it is a planetary leak of the temporal portals that govern the strata, above and below ground, as rock, ocean and atmosphere. The accumulation of more and more things on the surface relies on burrowing further and further into the depths of the earth and *de*sedimenting its stratal flows to release temporal mixing at the material level (predominantly as geochemical and heat exchanges). The *Nature* report raises alarms about the weight of the human 'footprint' on Earth – the 'heavy' mammalian supremacy – as a planetary homogenising condition, but is depicted as socially indifferent to the uneven geographies, racial inequalities and health disparities that situate the relations and exchanges between the underground and surface and between the surface and atmosphere.

As a cartographical proposition to map the geosocial exchanges and affective architectures of extraction, this article develops the notion of *planetary portals*, in order to move through three seemingly disparate sites, in which the vertical and the diasporic geographies of material and social life might become visible, as they cross thresholds. The conceptual history of the portal in speculative writing and science-fiction, where it often represents an opening into time and space that connects seemingly unconnected geographies, offers a theoretical innovation for unearthing the racialised logics of extractive capitalism. The planetary itself and its material transformation of the planet is a portal of racial capitalism. Our aim here is to invoke the portal as a temporal splice in time and space that bends the imagined connections between places, and enables us to think with the changes in state that exceed territory and transform planetarity.

Aerial Haulage, Kimberley Mine.

Right: Colesberg Kopje, Kimberley, South Africa, 1873.

Opposite: Aerial haulage, Kimberley Mine, South Africa, 1900s.

The portal and the portal

In architectural and urban design discourses, portals often refer to 'gateways' that serve as a passage between places, and which come to 'mark the point of transition' between discrete and bounded spaces.[5] For portal designs to be considered successful, they must provide an affective shift in the experience of the subject from one of movement to that of arrival, from that of becoming to that of being.[6] Portals have a 'gravitational pull' that entices, invites – that sucks! – the subject into a hole, with an almost 'alchemical quality', bestowing upon the city a 'hole' lot of 'mystery and magic'.[7] To the architect, the portal is more than just a conduit, it is a place in its own right; a 'solid thing'[8] that harnesses the affective powers of that gravitational pull towards somewhere beyond. Yet, the mysterious alchemy of harnessing that pull is inconspicuously indifferent to social inequalities that result from the uneven geochemical and racialised geographies of the urban environment. As Sara Ahmed argues, architects and urban designers often explain how the built environment acquires its form by considering *what* it is made useful for, and thus inviting socio-cultural assumptions that homogenise and standardise considerations of *who* it is made useful for.[9] How might the portal bring architectural discourse towards ways of reckoning with the politics that undergird the affective powers of the push and pull in and out of the portal hole?

We invoke the portal as a disruptive method that pinches, pulls and rips the idea of the 'planetary' as an event surface and sets the conditions for imagining the transitory stages of anthropocenic planetary processes that are gathered under the rubric of 'the Anthropocene'. We bring together geographical ideas of disruptive upside-down surfaces to collaborators in architecture, design and earth science in order to reimagine society and space as actively involved in the racialised geopolitics of 'changing states' through the proliferations of inversions, depletions and dispersals. Engaging the portal as method, we propose that the 'planetary' is spatially and temporally produced through geographic and racial inequalities that have their histories in colonialism, slavery and neo-extractivism.[10] For example, miners descend into the world's deepest mines in South Africa to extract precious metals and stones that are sold on London and New York's Stock Exchange, extending the legacies of Cecil Rhodes (in the vehicle of De Beers) and the affective architectures of British colonial occupation of South Africa. This 'colonialism beyond colonialism' hints at both the afterlife of migratory extraction forms (the plantation, the mine, the 'racialised poor') and the continued portals of transference of value to concentrated nodes of power. *Who* descends and *what* floats is an affectual racialised geography of depth and inversion that tells geostories about the historical exchanges of materialities of earth and capital in planetary transformation. The statues may be gone or coming down (#rhodesmustfall), but the racialised geophysics of extraction remains.

In the following, we move through three planetary portals – the mine, the skyscraper and the data centre – to produce a cartography of material affluences, exchanges of materials and temporal effluent that simultaneously circulate, escape and are sedimented into the spaces of the mine, the skyscrapers and the data centres. These planetary portals draw attention to the ways that material affluences aren't necessarily captured and don't always materialise, but instead come to hover, floating in a tortured state of endless grind and incompleteness that nevertheless materialises on specific racialised persons and sites.

Planetary Portals in the Upside-Down World

Sammy Baloji, The Tower, 7th Street, Quartier Industriel, municipality of Limete, Kinshasa, 2015.

The high-rise

The proliferation of high-rise developments across the African continent is evident in the extensive erection of billboards, adorned with CGI announcing the arrival of gleaming steel and glass towers. From Johannesburg to Kinshasa, from Douala to Nairobi, the allure of spectacular skylines and the aspirational economies that verticality engenders create a fantasy of inclusion into a vision of growth and prosperity;[11] a fantasy that places the skyscraper as the penultimate marker of 'progress', assuring the viewer that African cities are about to join the global elite of 'world-class' cities;[12] constituting an 'ocular ground' where the image representing the thing is as good as the thing itself.[13] The allure of 'progress' that is associated with vertical ascent is, as critics remark, entangled in and corrupted by an unregulated construction market and poor-quality housing that exposes the social failures and consequences of questionable governance practices and inadequate upkeep.[14]

In Nairobi, for example, Smith shows how the regular collapse of residential towers, as a result of poor-quality construction and local government corruption, gives rise to the idea of 'fake' towers – not as opposed to 'real' towers, but referring to the poorer quality of counterfeit products that are sold and consumed at lower cost for convenience. Just as fake designer bags, fake Coca-Cola or fake medicine allow the buyer to own the idea of the 'real', the 'fake' tower is a dreamscape that keeps the investor or occupant hovering in mid-air, speculating the potential return on investment. *The highrise as hustle.*

In Kinshasa, de Boeck draws attention to the unfinished high-rise building known as 'The Docteur's Tower', which embodies the desire for an idea that in essence is unrealisable. Ideated and funded by the medical doctor known locally simply as 'Docteur', the tower is meant to house a vertical community, including a hospital on the ground floors, offices for lawyers and visiting scientists and artists, an aviation school, a communal restaurant for residents, and Docteur's own domicile at the summit, a spire that brings people closer to God. From the medical healing of the body at ground level to the spiritual healing of the soul at the top, the tower is a spire from which to aspire – an architectural materialisation of the simulated realities that are floated in financial and physical space only 'before plunging back into the chaos of the surrounding city'.[15]

The crumbling, material realities of these vertical fantasies constitute a 'vertical optics' that,

Left: Kyubo, 1898. Geodetic marker at the Kyubo Falls.

Right: Sammy Baloji, Lupiri Lua Baluba, 2010. Remnants of a geodetic marker. The markers were destroyed under the pretext that they covered ore treasures hidden by the Belgians. In this image: Mwenze Augustin (chief Mpanga's grandson) and Seya Faustin.

as Simone suggests, 'obscures the messiness on the ground … underneath it'.[16] The high-rise engenders an 'ocular politics' of illusion, a false promise of 'minimal interference from the larger city'.[17] 'High life' cannot disassociate itself from the chaotic unruliness of the city's streets and back alleys, from the ground on which it stands and from which it aims to take flight – as James Baldwin reminds us: 'Whatever goes up must come down.'[18]

The mine

As we let the gravitational pull carry us closer towards the ground, another lustrous, oblong object pierces the planetary. In the popular meme 'how it started/how it's going', London rapper Lowkey draws attention to the origin stories of the new iPhone, and the earthed conditions of mining that deliver the smooth and shiny into our networks and affective communicative architectures. Drawing attention to the material base of the networked computational base is not indeed new,[19] yet the reach of its transformation of planetary states, its intervention in architectures of material affect, far exceed the infrastructures and sites of extraction. Drawing attention to the 'paleontological condition of media',[20] Jennifer Gabrys suggests we see electronics as 'fossilized commodities'.[21] As commodity chain analysis and ethical sourcing try to fix the production 'life', the 'end of life' dematerialising of electronics remains at best aspirational and instead suggests that 'these fossil forms are instead evidence of more complex and contingent material events'.[22] Through the narrative promise of dematerialisation, the racialised miner remains as a stubborn figure of and in the earth, resolutely unable to float or rise above the dirt. The mine makes Franz Fanon's *Wretched of the Earth* eternal.

The iPhone 12 is now equipped with a LiDAR scanner as part of the camera function, to effectively measure distance and depth of materialities using lasers.

The same technology established the representational genre and grammars of identification of rare earth metals, as well as fuels and materials for extraction, by producing 3D underground maps of environments and distinct material traces of the elusive materialities. As the first phone to employ the sophisticated LiDAR technology, the iPhone 12 is a miniaturised version of the macro transformative technologies of extraction that are transforming earth, geopolitical and subjective states. The phone has a recursive relation to its larger,

Below: Cross-section of the Kimberley Mine, 1887.

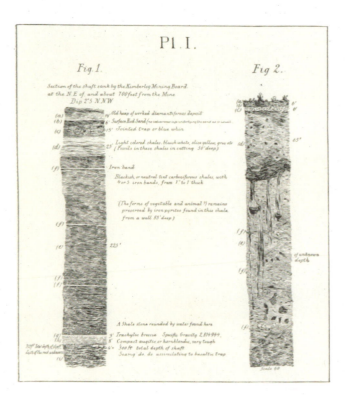

Working at the Intersection: Architecture After the Anthropocene

planetary transformations, operating as a domestic portal. The critical minerals that LiDAR is used to detect are crucial to the smart cities and urban infrastructures that propel the dreaming of the green smart city and its 'idiot subjects'.[23] 'Seeing through the surface' as LiDAR technologies promise in their topographical mapping of geology sets up the conditions of how the underground becomes visible and verticality is rendered in service to the surface.

This geosocial formation[24] enacts a telescoping effect whereby the technologies of detection and their bounty become miniaturised in the very digital technologies that drive the conditions of extraction in the first instance. A domestic portal in your pocket. The mine is the archetype of colonial portals; the undergrounded racialised periphery that feeds the centre. And, its extractive type proliferates out in a microcosm of pocket portalism that adheres to other spatialities of extraction, even as the mine continues to underpin the material infrastructures that support its ongoing circulation, as a planetary blueprint for unequal exchange.

The data server centre
'It is the engine of the internet', 'a giant building with a lot of power, a lot of cooling and a lot of computers', 'row upon row of machines'. These quotes introduce a rather dated 2014 tour of the Google data server centre located in North Carolina, 'one node in a larger network', uploaded to YouTube. It is one of many similar videos available across the internet taking viewers inside the wonders of the data server centre of prominent technology companies and the adjoining industries of DCIM (data centre infrastructure management) and securitisation. Tours usually start from the drone perspective of hovering above a benign-looking one-storey building sprawling out across peri-urban landscapes that could be anywhere really. Location does not matter in the replication of data server centres (bland homogeneity is the point). The servers, we learn, are encased in a vault protected by several gates of biometric security starting at the perimeter of the campus and edging inwards to form an ever-tighter enclosure around the actual server halls. We follow employees as they surrender iris, fingerprint and facial information and step into portals that perform a full body scan before exiting them on the other side. The portal in this instance exhibits the iconography of science-fiction. It is a tall glass tube that opens via sliding doors that wrap around the central cylinder and lock the body into a tight space while electromagnetic radiation is used to scan for concealed rogue objects. The portal is a bridge to the inviolable server hall.

Natural light recedes as we pass through the security threshold and into a vast room with bundles of thick piping, imbricating ceiling and walls; air vents poke down on row upon row of the black-boxed hardware that is stacked high on mesh shelving. The monotonous hum of data server centres and their distinct lack of character gives way to the notion that they represent sublime technology similar to that recorded by Nye.[25] American cultural identity, Nye argued, fizzes in the collective effervescence induced from standing atop the Empire State building and gazing out across the canyon streets of New York City, in awe of the conjoining of human and environment. The server centre connects to no such experience and nor does it offer a majestic view across the plateaus of technoscience.[26] The grandeur of the technological sublime is in the endlessly flashing lights that, like REM sleep, dart here and there, signalling a reticulated world of virtual activity. As portals to the dreamscapes of the digit, data server centres perform a kind of mind/body separation, an idealised dematerialisation, that justifies tours in the first place – not much is known about data server centres, and even Google's own developers struggle to comprehend 'where the internet lives'.[27] The realisation that servers do exist in very material and techno-political infrastructures feels like a horrid tug down to earth that is resisted by the buoyancy of sublimated digital dreamscapes.

The mind or mental activity of data server centres, so to speak, is epistemologically valorised and commercialised in the space-time compressions of global digital infrastructures. The flashing lights signify the quantification of informational exchange that forms the economic resource of the technology industry. The server centre is a mine, in which the infrastructural space that Easterling detects, composed of arrangements of human and non-human objects dancing across an informational plane, is excavated for data that is then aggregated to generate surplus profit.[28] Sped-up footage of containerisation, global factory shop floors, financial transactions, cloudbusting skyscrapers, city streets and ports of all kinds run through the mind when thinking about the choreographies of infrastructural space. These flashing images of planetary motion represent a diminished corpus of geosocial histories through which the ethics of data production in its current material manifestation are brought into question. A kind of 'ruinous vitalism' runs underneath data server centres as they expand like farms across the Global North – the southern hemisphere is too hot to cool data centres effectively and does not represent key markets of giant tech companies.[29] While data server centres provide the cloud storage for more sophisticated and condensed forms of digitisation and algorithmic calculation extending into all spheres of society, ruination occurs in the material infrastructures that racialise and subvert other bodies in its service.

     A portal opens up in revealing connections between bodies and data in the histories of mining. Data server centres rely on prosumptive forms of human labour as the key resource; to swipe, like, tweet, photograph, geotag, shop, travel, talk, etc. makes money, when aggregated. The mineral mines that provision the building of data server centres, and the fossilised electronic commodities they vitalise, were historically also sites of colonial medicine and maternal health invested in monitoring the replication of a labour force to work in the mine.[30] Census data, reproductive medicine and paperwork converge in the African mine, making it into an implement of surveillance in the colonial state. There are gendered implications to this surveillance strategy in which African women's bodies were subjected to experimentation and exploitation in the codification of the womb as a mimetic device. The skyscraper, the mine and the data server centres might present the refracted mirror images of each other; yet, the ideologies of colonial and reproductive medicine remain continuous in how human bodies are coded and decoded as rather straightforward informational resources and users.[31] This rendering of corporeal existence negates all those 'middling figures',[32] the odd incongruous entities that traverse boundaries of the material and immaterial and form strange lexicons through which such seamless interpretations of the dematerialised floating body are made possible and mobilised at the planetary level, at the same time providing grammars of impossibility, stubborn resilience and survivalism.[33]

A floater!

Resistance and survivalism come in various forms. In Kinshasa, for example, it seems there is too much resistance across the city's modern, colonial infrastructures caused by potholes and sinkholes that after heavy rainfall leave the city surfaces scarred, exposing 'colonialism's broken infrastructural dreams'.[34] *Boda bodas* (the motorcycle taxis) sometimes disappear down potholes after the rains if they are not forewarned. It can be difficult to discern the dangerous depths of the pools of red muddy waters that pockmark busy streets.

Kimberley Mine – middle stage, South Africa, 1875.

The *bodas* exemplify Simone's 'people as infrastructure'.[35] In cities across East Africa, they provide cheap public transportation capable of weaving through the jam, and, as a social group of predominantly young men, they also codify the city in order to navigate its dangerous potholes and pitfalls, or in some cases to exploit them.

While the infrastructural inertia of the hole threatens to suck bodies into a vortex of urban vulnerability, Kinois[36] actively resist the gravitational pull of the portal hole through a range of enunciative practices that ridicule the sink-logic of failed colonial dreams. Enthused with sophisticated irony, Kinois transform Kinshasa's holes into gathering spaces that sustain informal shadow economies and offer respite from the delimiting conditions of the urban; underground nightclubs, dive bars, drinking places and dance pubs that all echo the same chorus: 'if we have to live in a hole, we might as well dance in it!'.[37] In other words, the vortex of vulnerability is transformed into a dreamlike dancescape where desires and fears intermingle in an indulgent state where everything floats. Potholes become portholes, become portals for opening up new ways of rewriting the hi/stories and geographies of the planetary – ways that pinch, puncture, rip and rupture the vertical hierarchies of planetary urbanisation.

Across a number of works by Pascale Marthine Tayou, verticality features as a central axis across which the viewer travels between the material world and the imaginary. *The Falling House* (2014) displays a wooden cabin with a corrugated tin roof hanging upside-down, suspended from the ceiling. This house is not a home, but the idea of one, a dreamlike 'encounter' with one. At closer inspection the viewer discovers that the wooden walls are overlayered with photographs and discarded objects that, with their ghostly appearances haunt the house and keep the viewer hovering in mid-air, somewhere between the familiar and the strange. In Tayou's upside-down world the viewer does not defy gravity but is forced to walk around the house or crawl under it in order to circumvent its obstruction of movement. The bodily manipulation sends the viewer hurtling into a fall. In the same way that our dreams are onset by falling into sleep, the house is falling and it pulls the viewer with it; drags or sucks the body into its gravitational vortex.

This world of upside-down hovers ambivalently between the different ways we might understand and experience the fall; lingering between falling in love and falling apart, between tripping and tripping. *The Falling House* is a conduit for floating between our uncontrollable desires and destructive forces, between the intimate attachments we forge to others and the dark attenuations of these kinds of attachment.[38] Like the enunciative informalisation of the holes that scar the urban landscape in Kinshasa, Tayou's upside-down world is not just a conduit, but a jolt that sends you falling into the world anew, creating a rupture, an opening for alternate ways of composing, compiling and configuring urban life. Tayou's planetary portal provides the push and pull that Kathleen Stewart suggests has come to dominate the affective dimensions of our very ordinary lives, making floating a condition of possibility:

Things have started to float.
It's as if solid ground has given way, leaving us hanging like tender cocoons suspended in a dream world. As if the conditions and possibilities of a life have themselves begun to float ... there's no denying that it has a buoyancy too. A vibrancy alive with gamblers, hoarders, addicts and shopping malls.[39]

The compulsion to dance, to let the geochemical infusion of the planetary portal carry you into that riskful state of floating, with glamour and buoyancy, to rise above the whirlpools of breakdown, while the fire burns here and elsewhere! As financial architectures keep moving the money and shifting the accumulative sites of value, they produce the polluting effluence of their disappeared presence. Thus, environmental and social justice is constantly being displaced through the planetary changes in state as well as those 'on the ground'. Dispossession is pinched through the portal of exchange. Environmental justice is in the immediate and the dispersed. Spatial justice mediates across vertical states and racialised undergrounds. Climate justice haunts atmospheres that arrive without accountability. Portals are an analytic that bring attention to the severance of space and time over more than physical geography; they call attention to geosocial states of material worlds and the transformation of affective architectures. 'Dying to Live!' as one South African newspaper[40] has it, on the 'dark underground world' of survival for the *zama zamas* (illegal miners). The methodology and theory of portals exposes what Doreen Massey called the 'power geometries' of space, adding a cartography of dispersal that brings together the disparate processes that connect across the planetary, crossing boundaries and states of matter, changing states as an affectual planetary infrastructure of the upside-down world.

Sammy Baloji, *Détail site d'extraction artisanale #2*, 2011, 2012.

1. Gray Brechin, *Imperial San Francisco: Urban Power, Earthly Ruin*, Berkeley, University of California Press, 1999.
2. Gavin Bridge, 'The hole world: Scales and spaces of extraction', *Scenario Journal 05: Extraction*, para. 5 and 13, https://scenariojournal.com/article/the-hole-world, 2015.
3. The notion of 'buried sunshine' refers to the compressed solar power that seeps from carboniferous depots and reservoirs underground, and is taken from Timothy Mitchell, *Carbon Democracy*, London, Verso, 2011, p12.
4. Emily Elhacham, et al., 'Global human-made mass exceeds all living biomass', *Nature*, vol. 588, no. 7838, pp442–4, https://doi.org/10.1038/s41586-020-3010-5, 2020.
5. Christopher Alexander, et al., *A Pattern Language: Towns, Buildings, Construction*, New York, Oxford University Press, 1977, p278.
6. Edward T White, 'Path-portal-place', in Matthew Carmona and Steve Tiesdell, eds, *Urban Design Reader*, Oxford, Architectural Press, 1989, pp185–98, p188.
7. Ibid., p188.
8. Alexander, et al., *A Pattern Language*, p278.
9. Sara Ahmed, *What's the Use? On the Uses of Use*, London and Durham, 2019.
10. Kathryn Yusoff, *A Billion Black Anthropocenes or None*, Minneapolis, University of Minnesota Press, 2018.
11. Filip De Boeck and Sammy Baloji, *Suturing the City: Living Together in Congo's Urban Worlds*, London, Autograph ABP, 2016; Constance Smith, 'Collapse fake buildings and gray development in Nairobi', *Focaal*, no. 86, pp11–23, https://doi.org/10.3167/fcl.2020.860102, 2020.
12. Zoë Goodman, '"Going vertical" in times of insecurity: Constructing proximity and distance through a Kenyan gated high-rise', *Focaal*, no. 86, pp24–35, https://doi.org/10.3167/fcl.2020.860103, 2020; Mpho Matsipa, 'Woza! Sweetheart! On braiding epistemologies on Bree Street', *Thesis Eleven*, vol. 141, no. 1, pp31–48, https://doi.org/10.1177/0725513617720241, 2017; Smith, 'Collapse fake buildings and gray development in Nairobi'.
13. McCarthy, quoted in Boeck and Baloji, *Suturing the City*, p246.
14. AbdouMaliq Simone, 'People as infrastructure: Intersecting fragments in Johannesburg', *The People, Place, and Space Reader*, vol. 16, no. 3, pp241–6, https://doi.org/10.4324/9781315816852, 2004; Constance Smith and Saffron Woodcraft, 'Introduction: Tower block "failures"? High-rise anthropology', *Focaal*, no. 86, 2020, pp1–10, https://doi.org/10.3167/fcl.2020.860101; Elisa Tamburo, 'High-rise social failures regulating technologies, authority, and aesthetics in the resettlement of Taipei military villages', *Focaal*, no. 86, 2020, pp36–52, https://doi.org/10.3167/fcl.2020.860104.
15. Boeck and Baloji, *Suturing the City*, p220.
16. AbdouMaliq Simone, *Jakarta: Drawing the City Nearer*, Minneapolis, Minnesota Press, 2014, p63.
17. Ibid.
18. James Baldwin, 'The fire next time', in *Baldwin: Collected Essays*, ed. by Toni Morrison, New York, The Library of America, 1963, p346.
19. Jennifer Gabrys, *Digital Rubbish: A Natural History of Electronics*, Ann Arbor, MI, University of Michigan Press, 2011.
20. Ibid., pv.
21. Ibid., p7.
22. Ibid., p7.
23. Jennifer Gabrys, *Program Earth: Environmental Sensing Technology and the Making of a Computational Planet*, Minneapolis, University of Minnesota Press, 2016, pp206–38.
24. Nigel Clark and Kathryn Yusoff, 'Geosocial formations and the Anthropocene', *Theory, Culture and Society*, vol. 34, nos. 2–3, pp3–23, https://doi.org/10.1177/0263276416688946, 2017.
25. David E Nye, *American Technological Sublime*, Cambridge, MA, MIT Press, 1996.
26. Kathryn Yusoff, *Geologic Life: Inhuman Intimacies and the Geophysics of Race*, vol. 111, no. 3, pp663–76, 2021.
27. Jennifer Holt and Patrick Vonderau, '"Where the internet lives": Data centres as cloud infrastructure', in Lisa Parks and Nicole Starosielski, eds, *Signal Traffic: Critical Studies of Media Infrastructures*, Champaign, IL, University of Illinois Press, 2015, pp71–93.
28. Keller Easterling, *Extrastatecraft: The Power of Infrastructure Space*, London and New York, Verso, 2014.
29. M Wilhelm-Solomon, 'The ruinous vitalism of the urban form: Ontological orientations in inner-city Johannesburg', *Critical African Studies*, vol. 9, no. 2, 2017, pp174–91.
30. N Kretzmar, 'An introduction to the history of medicine on the diamond fields of Kimberley, South Africa', *Medical History*, vol. 18, no. 2, 1974, pp155–62; Nancy Rose Hunt, *A Colonial Lexicon: Of Birth Ritual, Medicalisation and Mobility in the Congo*, Durham, NC, Duke University Press, 1999.
31. Kretzmar, 'An introduction to the history of medicine on the diamond fields of Kimberley, South Africa'.
32. Hunt, *A Colonial Lexicon*, p2.
33. Simone, 'People as infrastructure: Intersecting fragments in Johannesburg', *Public Culture 1*, Durham, NC, Duke University Press, vol. 16, no. 3, 2004, https://doi.org/10.12.15/08992363-16-3-407.
34. Boeck and Baloji, *Suturing the City*, p222.
35. Simone, 'People as infrastructure: Intersecting fragments in Johannesburg'.
36. Residents of Kinshasa are known as Kinois.
37. Boeck and Baloji, *Suturing the City*, p223.
38. Lauren Berlant, *Cruel Optimism*, Durham, NC, Duke University Press, 2011.
39. Kathleen Stewart, *Ordinary Affects*, Durham and London, Duke University Press, 2007, p61.
40. Kamohelo Mohapi, 'Dying to live! People's paper takes you underground with zama zamas...', *Daily Sun*, South Africa, 19 June 2014, pp1–2.

From Anthropocene to Biocene

Novel Bio-Integrated Design as a Means to Respond to the Current Biodiversity and Climate Crisis

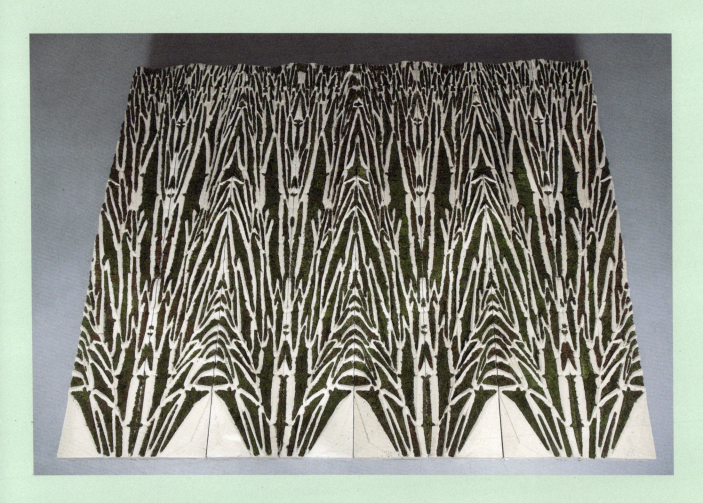

Marcos Cruz and Brenda Parker

Bioreceptive concrete wall with transplanted moss for the exhibition La Fabrique du Vivant at the Centre Pompidou (eight panels made of porous TecCast), 2019.

Our planet is in an epoch of disequilibrium. Unsustainable anthropocentric models of growth, production and habitat are creating unjustifiable social inequalities, depleting our finite resources and leading to the destruction of our environment. We have disrupted biogeochemical cycles, the key processes mediated by microorganisms and plants for the maintenance of our atmosphere, our soils and availability of clean water.[1] In the short term, our highest priority is to reduce emissions to stem climate change. But with global populations expected to raise to a breathtaking 10.9 billion in 2100[2] and our building stock to double by 2050,[3] we don't know how our long-term future will look. How will design processes have to change if we are to guarantee our long-term survival on the planet?

Defining bio-integrated design

Bio-integrated design is a novel discipline that takes this question as the departure point for a radical new vision of how we will design our future human habitat. It draws together two key phenomena: biology as the dynamic and complex product of billions of years of evolution, and us humans, who through our agency and activities continue to transform our planet. Bio-integrated design puts forward a holistic approach emergent from the intersection of working methods from the applied arts and sciences. This requires a set of epistemic tools that draw from the research culture of biotechnology[4] and the embedded abductive reasoning and aesthetic consideration of design. Therefore, it encompasses diverse groups of expertise – architects and biochemical engineers, but also botanists, ecologists, planners, social scientists and artists – working together to create new forms of human settlement that emerge from the repercussions of the climate, biodiversity and soil crises. Bio-integrated design derives its core principles of sustainability from the respective disciplinary foundations[5][6] and seeks to establish meaningful modes of production.[7] We need to urgently move beyond the destructive impact of the Anthropocene and find a way back to our biological origins and create an integrated system where newly conceived human habitats feed from the inexhaustible resources of sunlight, carbon and water. The profound change needed to address our existential predicament calls for a new transdisciplinary approach to the hyperobject[8] of climate change, using hybrid design, scientific and socially engaged methods to produce new architectural typologies and new ways of living in and with nature.

Distinct from what is now commonly termed *biodesign* – implying processes that are mostly product- and art-oriented – biologically integrated design embraces a wider variety of outputs that range from systems design and material production to the conception of smaller objects, spaces and buildings, with implications on an urban and territorial scale. Bio-integrated design addresses bigger questions shaped by biotechnology, computation and data-driven technologies, architecture and the environment, along with socio-cultural dynamics. To start with, the challenge is how we can realistically achieve a carbon-positive built environment where the basic building blocks are made of new bio-based composites with the expressive and functional diversity of current materials. While this is primarily a technical question in which 'form-follows-material',[9] it also needs to be understood in the context of a much-needed paradigm shift from traditional aesthetic values obsessed with purity and perfection to embrace new impure aesthetics[10] applied to the design for ageing buildings.[11] While we have to value the heterogeneity and imperfection of future materials, we also need to stop cleansing and manicuring our landscape and buildings in order to incorporate the unpredictable properties of time and decay, and the vulnerability of a new soft and biologically driven materiality. Bio-fabrication procedures, on the other hand, are creating disruptive modes of manufacture that promote equitable supply chains. Viscous materials – from cellulose or clay-based composites to chitosan and polymer-based hydrogel – are being robotically extruded, employing multifunctional and multi-material processes[12] to create scaffolds and substrates that can embed living matter.[13] Inherent to bio-integrated design is the role of the living. Biology plays a central role here, that goes beyond being a simple environmental regulator, model or inspiration; biology is in itself the medium of a multi-layered design approach that is not only materially but also socially integrated.

As designers, we need to adopt biocentric working modes, forging new habits and systems of dwelling and production that reconnect us humans to other species and our surroundings. In this context, photosynthetic organisms are fundamental. Existing in every biome of our planet, they utilise abundant yet simple starting materials of sunlight, carbon dioxide and water, and by generating inherently benign waste products they offer a highly adapted and decentralised – and thus equitable – resource that is accessible to all. Phototrophic production of materials and structures is a strategy to reduce the embodied water and energy footprints of our surroundings; this suggests a different approach to how we should design.

Anthropogenic mass,[14] especially in the form of ubiquitous buildings and infrastructure, has already created a vast range of new environments and artificial surface area. Human-made constructions offer a colossal scaffold for autotrophic organisms in which they can be integrated, or exhibit evolutionary adaptation towards these contemporary habitats. The selection pressure exerted by our built environment may even give rise to novel speciation as in the case of specific lichens in old churchyards or other ancient constructions.[15] In this manner, bio-integrated design arises from the interfacial properties of materials, organisms and their surroundings. The result is emergent hybrid technologies that generate radically new environments infused with natural and synthetic living forms. Cities covered with small-scale growth photosynthesising without any maintenance, or plants proliferating indoors creating a new diverse microbiome that sustains our wellbeing and health will offer us a new biogenic setting in which to live. We will also be able to compute and program buildings that will grow into habitable spaces with self-regulated and self-healing qualities. Whether rural aggregates or large-scale conurbations, human settlements will integrate photosynthetic systems on multiple scales and levels to generate food and power, and remediate our water and air, while creating a much-needed carbon sink and producing oxygen to breathe. Our future photosynthetic human habitat will become an active participant in the global nutrient cycles, helping to abate climate change. Through bio-integrated design we will be able to make our future habitats embody the conceptual and technological shift from our short-lived Anthropocene to a much longer-lived Biocene.

According to the United Nations (UN 73rd General Assembly), we only have until 2030 to prevent irreversible damage from climate change. To address these major challenges, radically new design-led processes that are underpinned by a solid scientific and cultural structure need to be implemented. Beside laboratory-based testing and community engagement, physical constructions are required to be trialled to materialise this future vision for the built environment. Projects are being first upscaled from lab work to a level of prototype feasibility, so that we can implement, monitor and calibrate the projects to produce viable outcomes that can be applied across different contexts. To contextualise the application of bio-integrated design, here we will discuss a number of bottom-up manifestations of this to modify and augment our existing built environment.

Poikilohydric Living Wall: manufacturing and testing of bioreceptive panels at Pennine Stone Limited and site installation at St Anne's Catholic Primary School, London, 2018–20.

Above left: Digital microscopy of moss ecologies and substrates within bioreceptive materials, 2020–1
Above right: Biomineralised samples of ELM with hydrogel, silica aggregate and Oscillatoria animalis cyanobacteria.

Bioreceptivity, microbiome and embedded ecologies

The concept of bioreceptivity is central to the concept of the photosynthetic human habitat. It underpins the creation of new types of poikilohydric designs[16] where externally exposed facades with incorporated small-scale plants are able to switch on and off their photosynthetic activity according to the availability of water. Without additional irrigation and maintenance, the surfaces are bio-colonised with drought-resistant cryptogrammic species that are self-regenerative, leading to more sustainable forms of greening in cities. For this, current studies are demonstrating the importance of semi-organic substrates and the role of bacteria in promoting hormonally induced growth, which is important when establishing and embedding new plant communities on vertical surfaces. To support these humic substrates, different aggregates such as sand, cork or other recycled materials are being tested to evaluate and calibrate the porosity and biochemical set-up on components on which photosynthesising organisms can proliferate. Also, particular morphological patterns are crucial to increase the absorption and retention of water, while offering completely new ornamental qualities to buildings. Algae, mosses, lichens and small-scale ferns are able to absorb pollutants while being hugely important in the uptake of nitrogen and carbon, creating new ecologies that form an inconspicuous green continuum in cities.

Going beyond the macro-scale interventions of green infrastructure networks, it is within the remit of bio-integrated design to consider the ecology of the microbiome of our homes and cities. The role of biodiversity of microbial actors is now being shown to have important implications on ecosystem services as well as plant, invertebrate and human health. The integrative system of Microbiome-Inspired Green Infrastructure (MIGI) has been proposed as an approach to promote healthy urban ecosystems. MIGI can be defined as nature-centric infrastructure that is restored and/or designed and managed to promote interactions between humans and environmental microbiomes, with explicit considerations for sustaining microbially mediated ecosystem functionality and resilience.[17] The importance of this is twofold – firstly to promote benefits to public health via improved immunoregulation, and secondly to enhance other microbially mediated processes for environmental benefit such as bioremediation, bioreceptivity and the biodiversity of ecosystems in cities, and vital repercussions for our overall future food security. MIGI invites designing for both human and non-human from the bottom up. For instance, embedding MIGI principles into new urban design requires a sensitivity to material selection in design and construction contexts in order to foreground environmental microbiota in a sociobiological context.[18]

Animate materials

Another fundamental task is to solve the unsustainability of current building materials. Biomineralisation offers a new path to grow rather than manufacture while reducing the environmental footprint of architectural materials.[19] Studies are showing that the use of filamentous cyanobacteria in a biocatalysis of calcium carbonate allows the production of a new type of engineered living material (ELM) with a structural integrity that can be used as a bulk solid for architecture. A variety of inert aggregates are mixed together with hydrogel, and photosynthetic organisms propagate three-dimensionally and bind particle aggregates. The use of phototrophic species that are capable of migrating towards light enables a high level of control and directionality of the biomineralisation process. Such photosynthetic organisms make use of inorganic carbon sources while also being poikilohydric and therefore capable of surviving built environment conditions. The resulting materials are regenerative when brought back to life and capable of self-healing, as well as being able to withstand periods of desiccation. The choice of aggregate creates semi-translucent conditions for light to penetrate. In addition, bioprecipitation processes enable the growth of biogenic veneers. These are extremely thin yet mechanically durable biofilms that offer an outer protection to structurally weaker bulk material within that can be lighter and/or less resistant to erosion and time. Moreover, biogenic veneers offer unique aesthetic properties that create nuances of structural colour and iridescence commonly found in living organisms such as mother-of-pearl. Current studies include walls clad with ceramic tiles that are being veneered with living microbial biofilms that self-assemble in a highly ordered three-dimensional manner. The resulting luminosity goes beyond the flatness of common material surfaces, presenting a new perceptual depth and radiance that is akin to some of the most valuable materials, such as amber, marble, onyx and gold. Biogenic silica-based composites are in fact living crusts that are synthesised in benign conditions, having the potential to actively participate in Earth's cycles by absorbing carbon and nitrogen. Applied across millions of square metres, they can mitigate the effects of climate change while offering truly novel aesthetic qualities to our cities.

Biogenic architecture in exhibition at the Kolektiv Gallery, Belgrade (2020) and Open Cell/ Biodesign Here Now, as part of London Design Week (2019).

Bio-digital workflows

To physically realise the vision of our future human habitat, new modes of simulation and production are being implemented in the design of bio-integrated systems. Advanced biocomputation and biofabrication combine self-generative processes with multi-physics simulations to allow for reciprocal testing and design protocols to achieve high-resolution living conditions. Variable parameters of viscosity, porosity or growth, for example, are being used to inform emergent design patterns, ultimately leading towards an unprecedented workflow and interrelationship between material properties, design, manufacturing and application. A research strand that is important in this context is focused on bioprinting of robotically extruded viscous materials to produce new living membranes. Immobilised terrestrial algae are being tested and calibrated to create highly three-dimensional hydrogel scaffolds that can absorb carbon and pollutants, while releasing oxygen to the environment for purpose-built facade panels. The use of computationally generated hierarchical fibrous patterns combined with additive manufacturing techniques offers an alternative approach to scale. In this approach, the contact of photosynthetic organisms is determined through the surface area. In contrast to systems relying on photobioreactor technology, such as in the BIQ house built in Hamburg in 2013 where gas and mass transfer limitations were overcome via mixing processes, the newly proposed interactions of cells and their environment are being facilitated by geometry. Immobilised systems thus offer a means of creating controlled microenvironments to support biological processes. Negotiating the role of water as 'both a liquid and solvent' as well the essential molecule for life[20] informs material selection, manufacturing and design application.[21]

Robotically extruded algae-laden hydrogel panel for the Tallin Architecture Biennale, Estonia, 2017.

Bio-integrated design's role in a molecular economy

Multiple bioregenerative protocols are being implemented to include the reuse and recycling of existing organic materials with the aim to contribute to a circular design strategy. Waste from the food processing industries and food spoilage ends up in landfills, representing a significant environmental problem today. The decomposition of food waste releases large quantities of methane, a greenhouse gas that is responsible for trapping heat in the atmosphere, significantly contributing to climate change. In response, novel lightweight and biodegradable composites extracted from specific food residues offer a potential low-cost and carbon-negative resource for the construction industry, mostly for interior spaces. Material explorations are being developed with a variety of cross-linking techniques and compositions to obtain desired properties in terms of material strength, hydrophobicity and viscosity. Beyond combating rising levels of waste, these materials address a shortage of raw material, while reducing embodied carbon costs in the built environment. Aimed at a variety of applications, complex geometric patterns are being robotically extruded and milled to create latticed structures for ceilings and walls.

A major legacy of our Anthropocene is the extraordinary levels of air and water pollution where the half-life of contaminants or the disturbance to ecosystems has been very severe. From the relatively recent yet widespread dispersion of microplastic waste, to the excavation of heavy metals from mining operations, a new Biocene will certainly be the epoch of long-term remediation. Bioremediation is a means of waste management method that implements biodegradation processes with physical, chemical and ecological characteristics of the contaminated sites to remove organic and inorganic pollutants. Employing biological mechanisms, in particular autotrophic organisms relying on relatively small inputs of exogenous nutrients, enables the creation of self-sustaining systems for remediation that has been explored within engineering design contexts.[22] While bioremediation is a platform for preventing future pollution, technologies often fail to translate, as the important link between the communities and the technological aspects is missing. Taking this as a departure point, low-tech ceramic wall tiles made by local craftsmen are being designed with intricate geometric patterns in which high-tech extrusion of hydrogels enables small-scale manufacturing with high levels of pollution, such as dye industries, to locally treat contaminated water. Pollutants such as cadmium can be sequestered by the algae-laden matrix,[23] reducing their distribution in water and soil.

In terms of energy, biophotovoltaics offer a decentralised and potentially revolutionary process in which light energy is converted into electrical energy by using photosynthetic ecologies of microorganisms. Certain microbial species are capable of a transfer of electrons outside the cell, a property known as exoelectrogenic activity. This has enabled the development of bioelectrochemical systems whereby living organisms directly generate electrical power, then are coupled to separate reductive processes. This has been demonstrated with communities of mosses and liquid-based photobioreactor systems to power small-scale modular systems for applications such as biosensors.[24] While present designs have been limited by the surface area of the anodic component, advances in material development are facilitating the design of such applications on a much larger scale for roofs or facades of buildings to generate meaningful amounts of clean energy.[25]

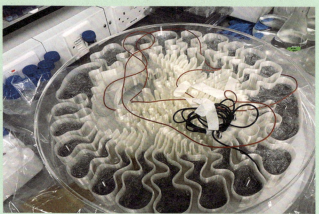

Working at the Intersection: Architecture After the Anthropocene

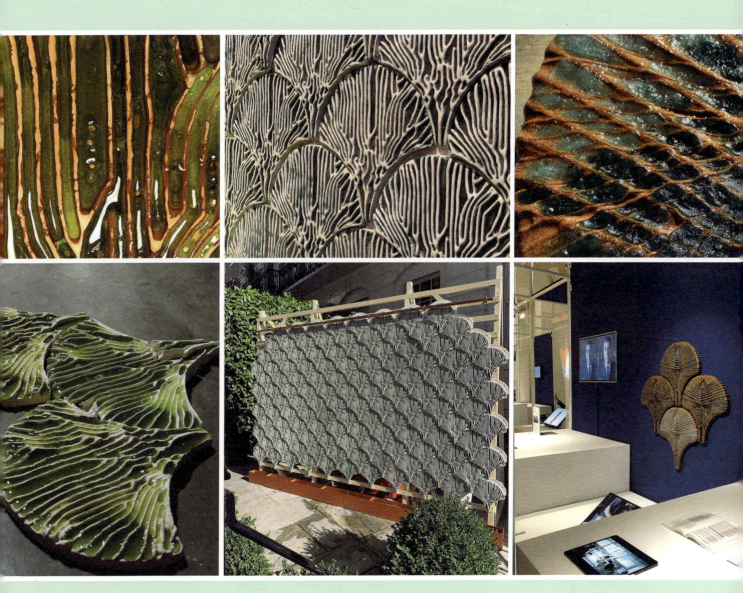

Opposite left: Robotically extruded food-waste composite.

Opposite right: Preparation of the biophotovoltaic component for the La Fabrique du Vivant exhibit at the Centre Pompidou, 2019; a 50cm Perspex dish contains aluminium anodic material in 3D printed form. © Schneel Malik

Above: INDUS 1.0 and 2.0 – a tile-based, modular bioreactor wall system for cleaning wastewater through bioremediation. Winner of the international Water Futures Design competition at A/D/O, New York, 2018. Installation exhibited at the Brompton Design District during London Design Week, 2019. Nominated for the Beazley Designs at the Design Museum, London, 2020. © Marcos Cruz and Schneel Malik

Perspectives beyond the Anthropocene
Considering the complementarity and integration of so many technologies results in future buildings becoming living and/or semi-living entities that fulfil architecture's path to an extended sense of ecology.[26] Tunable plant tissues represent an opportunity to have modifiable properties and controlled architectures.[27] Novel biomaterials and biofabrication protocols will define a new biosynthesis of living scaffolds that host an integrated vascularisation to permit the supply of nutrients and moisture to structures from within. To sustain the survival of cells the vascularisation of both cell scaffolds and tissue constructs applied on buildings is currently in the process of being scaled up. At the same time, the programming of cells will be necessary to allow a differentiation and controlled directionality of tissue growth to generate fully grown spaces able to be inhabited. Here, the intersection between tissue engineering, design and advances in robotic processes is pivotal for the development of what are highly complex morphologies that evolve and adapt over time with minimal input of resources and long-term maintenance.

In conclusion, moving beyond the short-lived Anthropocene demands the vision of a symbiotic co-existence of us humans with other species. Novel bio-integrated design methods offer a means to respond to the current biodiversity and climate crisis, and a way to create new living conditions that will emerge from the complex relationship between specific climates, cultural contexts and programmes, and the interfacial properties of materials and organisms. To accomplish this, pivotal research on future photosynthetic habitats requires a new epistemic culture based on co-creation and exchange between molecular, systems and synthetic biology; botany, ecosystems and urban ecologies; multifunctional composites and fabrication; design and urban space. With bio-integrated design, new scientific work methodologies embedded within design experimentation are leading to bioprocesses for meaningful scale-up. We are now finally witnessing a new sense of materiality and emergent hybrid biotechnologies that underpin the creation of a future human habitat infused with natural and synthetic living forms. The advent of the Biocene is in sight!

Screenshots of Prime Mover animation illustrating a future human habitat.

1. Ricardo Cavicchioli, et al., 'Scientists' warning to humanity: Microorganisms and climate change', *Nature Reviews Microbiology*, 2019, https://www.nature.com/articles/s41579-019-0222-5 2019, pp569–86.
2. United Nations, *World Population Prospects 2019: Highlights*, United Nations Publication, 2019.
3. IEA, *2019 Global Status Report for Buildings and Construction: Towards a Zero-Emissions, Efficient and Resilient Buildings and Construction Sector in International Energy Agency and the United Nations Environment Programme*, 2019.
4. Claes Gustafsson and Jordi Vallverdú, 'The best model of a cat is several cats', *Trends in Biotechnology*, vol. 34, no. 3, 2016, pp207–13.
5. Paul T Anastas and Julie B Zimmerman, 'Design through the 12 principles of green engineering', *Environmental Science and Technology*, 2003.
6. Victor J Papanek, *Design for the Real World: Human Ecology and Social Change*, St Albans, Paladin, 1974.
7. Ernst Friedrich Schumacher, *Small is Beautiful: A Study of Economics as if People Mattered*, London, Abacus, 1973.
8. Timothy Morton, *Ecology without Nature: Rethinking Environmental Aesthetics*, Cambridge, MA, Harvard University Press, 2007.
9. Marcos Cruz, 'Paramateriality: Novel biodigital manifolds', *Architectural Materialisms*, 2018, pp88–110.
10. Marcos Cruz and Richard Beckett, 'Bioreceptive design: A novel approach to biodigital materiality', *Architectural Research Quarterly*, vol. 20, no. 1, 2016, pp51–64.
11. Marcos Cruz, 'Design for ageing buildings: An applied research of poikilohydric living walls' in *The Routledge Companion to Contemporary Architectural History*, London, Routledge, 2021.
12. Steven Keating and Neri Oxman, 'Compound fabrication: A multi-functional robotic platform for digital design and fabrication', *Robotics and Computer-Integrated Manufacturing*, vol. 29, no. 6, 2013, pp439–48.
13. Shneel Malik, et al., 'Robotic extrusion of algae-laden hydrogels for large-scale applications', *Global Challenges*, vol. 4, no. 1, 2020, 1900064.
14. Emily Elhacham, et al., 'Global human-made mass exceeds all living biomass', *Nature*, vol. 588, no. 7838, 2020, pp442–4.
15. Oliver L Gilbert, *Lichens*, London, Collins, 2000, p151.
16. Marcos Cruz, *Poikilohydric Living Walls – a Bartlett Research Folio*, 2021.
17. Jake M Robinson, et al., *Microbiome-Inspired Green Infrastructure (MIGI): A Bioscience Roadmap for Urban Ecosystem Health*, in press, 2021.
18. Harry Watkins, et al., 'Microbiome-inspired green infrastructure: A toolkit for multidisciplinary landscape design', *Trends in Biotechnology*, 2020.
19. Nina Jotanovic, et al., 'The potential of biomineralization processes to reduce the environmental footprint of architectural materials', *ACS Sustainable Chemistry & Engineering*, in press, 2021.
20. Philip Ball, 'Water is an active matrix of life for cell and molecular biology', *Proceedings of the National Academy of Sciences*, vol. 114, no. 51, 2017, pp13327–35.
21. Shneel Malik, et al., 'Robotic extrusion of algae-laden hydrogels for large-scale applications', *Global Challenges*, vol. 4, no. 1, 2020, 1900064.
22. Lena I Fuldauer, et al., 'Managing anaerobic digestate from food waste in the urban environment: Evaluating the feasibility from an interdisciplinary perspective', *Journal of Cleaner Production*, no. 185, 2018, pp929–40; Christian J A Ridley, et al., 'Growth of microalgae using nitrate-rich brine wash from the water industry', *Algal Research*, no. 33, 2018, pp91–8.
23. Sergio Balzano, et al., 'Microalgal metallothioneins and phytochelatins and their potential use in bioremediation', *Frontiers in Microbiology*, 2020, p517.
24. Paolo Bombelli, et al., 'Electrical output of bryophyte microbial fuel cell systems is sufficient to power a radio or an environmental sensor', *Royal Society Open Science*, vol. 3, no. 10, 2016, 160249.
25. Christopher J Howe and Paolo Bombelli, 'Electricity production by photosynthetic microorganisms', *Joule*, vol. 4, no. 10, 2020, pp2065–9.
26. Marcos Cruz, 'Living buildings – architecture's path to ecology', TEDx talk, 2012, https://www.youtube.com/watch?v=YFKJW67X8hw.
27. Ashley L. Beckwith, et al., 'Tunable plant-based materials via in vitro cell culture using a *Zinnia elegans* model', *Journal of Cleaner Production*, no. 288, 2021, 125571.

Sitopia

A Landscape for Human and Non-Human Flourishing

Carolyn Steel

How shall we live in the future? In some ways, the question has never felt more open, yet in others it has never been more constrained. This contrast, between seemingly endless possibility and profound limitation, is the paradoxical condition of our age. In essence, it is a clash between our phenomenal technological prowess and the finite bearing capacity of our planet. The fact that some of us see the answer to this clash as the colonisation of other planets totally incapable of supporting any known form of life speaks volumes: at its most extreme, the technological mindset can lead us to the strangest of places; ones that almost make us forget what it means to be human.

So what *does* it mean to be human? While there are no easy answers to that question, it is nevertheless one which, as Descartes observed, marks us out as human simply by asking it. We are inhabitants of the Earth: conscious, living beings who evolved on the only planet known to sustain life, and, as far as we know, the only ones troubled by this fact. Our condition makes the question of how to live particularly challenging to address, which possibly explains why some prefer to imagine colonising Mars instead. Yet face it we must.

The question of how to live thus goes far beyond material considerations; it goes to the heart of who we think we are. And here, it seems, we are in a primal muddle. For roughly the past 2,500 years, our attempts to wrestle with the problem have evolved into two parallel strands – observational science and myth-making – creating a dualistic view of the world that seems to have reached a point of dysfunctional impasse. The US, for example, is a leading technological nation that has just successfully flown a helicopter on Mars, yet two in five Americans believe that the Earth was created in just seven days.[1] While cognitive dissonance on such a massive scale might be described as a coping strategy,

Chicago Union Stockyards, 1880. The opening up of the American Midwest to grain production made possible by the railroads gave rise to factory farming – feeding grain to cattle – and thus the invention of cheap meat.

THE GREAT UNION STOCK YARDS OF CHICAGO.

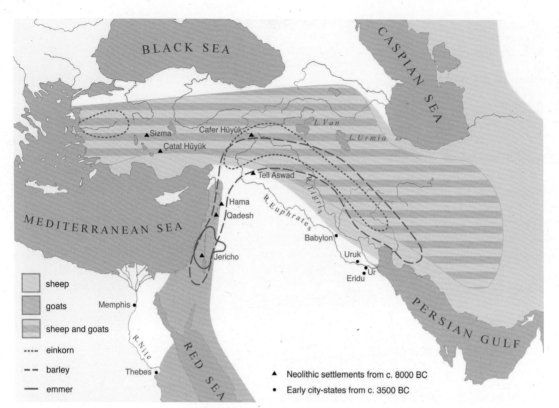

The Fertile Crescent, c. 3,500 BCE. The gradual adoption of farming as a primary means of subsistence in the ancient Near East led to the creation of static settlements, which eventually evolved into cities.

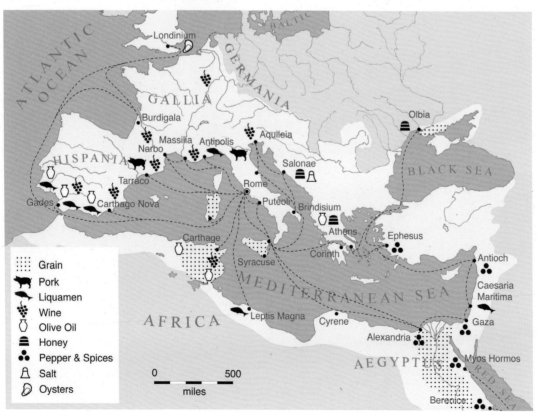

The food supply of ancient Rome. Rome relied on food imports from overseas from an early stage, thus pioneering the phenomenon we now know as 'food miles', in which cities are fed from distant lands.

it's scarcely helpful when it comes to grappling with urgent problems such as mass extinction or climate change. If we're going to create a future vision to which everyone can sign up, we're going to need to base it upon something undeniably real in which everyone has a stake. Such a medium is food.

Food occupies a unique place in our world, not only because we all need to eat, but because it sits at the nexus of our two most important relationships, with nature and one another. Food shapes our minds, bodies, homes, workplaces, politics, economics, cities, landscapes, environment and climate. Whether or nor not we realise it, we live in a world shaped by food; a place I call *sitopia* (from the Greek *sitos*, food + *topos*, place).[2] Since we don't value food, however, we live in a bad sitopia.

Living in a modern city, it can be hard to appreciate how fundamentally food shapes our world. Industrialisation has obscured the vital connections without which urban life would swiftly grind to a halt: the complex supply chains that bring our grain, oil, beans and sardines from the fields and seas where they are produced to our factories, supermarkets, cafes and kitchens. The foods on our plate are emissaries from other worlds; places that increasingly resemble a science-fiction nightmare rather than the rosy pictures we imagine. From vast feedlots and sheds full of tragic animals to monocultural grain fields harvested by drone-guided combines, huge trawlers dragging nets across seabeds or robotised production lines filleting fish at breakneck speed, the industrial spaces and processes that underpin our existence are as efficient as they are ruthless. In many ways, modern agri-food epitomises the fateful combination of technological capacity and ecological indifference that now threatens us and our planet.

Our modern way of life is based on the premise of cheap food. Yet, when you stop to think about it, no such thing could exist. Food consists of living things that we hunt or nurture and kill so that we can live. Food, in other words, is life; to cheapen it is to cheapen life itself. Yet, for the past two centuries, that is precisely what we've been doing. If the numerous externalities of industrial food – such as climate change, deforestation, mass extinction, pollution, water depletion, soil degradation, declining fish stocks, obesity, diet-related disease and zoonotic pandemics – were included in its price, such food would become instantly unaffordable, which, in a very real sense, it already is.

The Covid pandemic has shown the truth of this, revealing just how out of kilter our relationship with nature has become. Industrial farming has critically weakened biodiversity, while our increasing encroachment on wilderness exposes us to new disease. Experts have long warned of such dangers, yet it was only when supermarket shelves were stripped bare at the start of lockdown that the threat became real for many in the industrialised north. In that moment of panic, the illusion of easy plenty was shattered.

The shelves soon filled up again, but the underlying issues haven't gone away. On the contrary, their urgency has never been clearer. All of which raises the question: what would happen if we were to value food again? The answer is that there would be a revolution, not just in the way we eat, but in how we live. Since food connects every meaningful aspect of our existence, such a move is arguably the single most powerful thing we could do in order to transform our current way of life to make it far healthier, fairer and more resilient.

Urban paradox

Fortunately, there are plenty of clues as to how we might revalue food in our past, since the value of food was once obvious to everyone. Indeed, it would be no exaggeration to say that life in the pre-industrial era revolved around the question of how to eat. Feeding cities was particularly challenging, because not only did enough food have to be produced to feed urban populations, but it had to come to market in an edible state. For these reasons, grain has been the staple food of cities from the start, as it could be both produced in sufficient quantities and easily stored in order to feed people through the year.

The first to ponder the question of how to feed a city were the ancient Greeks. Both Plato and Aristotle grappled with the problem, concluding that the size of the *polis*, or city-state, was crucial: too small, and it would lack the resources to defend itself; too big, and it would struggle to feed itself from its own territory. The ideal arrangement was one in which every citizen had a house in the city and a farm in the countryside from which to feed it. Scaled up many times, such household management, or *oikonomia* (from *oikos*, household + *nemein*, management) would render the *polis* self-sufficient, its urban and rural regions in perfect balance. In his *Politics*, Aristotle went one step further, warning that *chrematistike*, the pursuit of wealth for its own sake, could bring ruin, since, unlike *oikonomia*, it had no natural limits.[3] One wonders what Aristotle would have made of our modern economics (a word derived from *oikonomia*), in which the pursuit of limitless wealth is the only goal.

Although few cities achieved the ideal self-sufficiency dreamed of by Plato and Aristotle, all did in fact practise some form of *oikonomia*. Most pre-industrial cities were highly productive, producing every sort of food that could be locally grown. Towns and cities were invariably surrounded by market gardens, orchards and vineyards, fertilised with liberal doses of 'night soil' (human and animal manure), carefully collected for the purpose. Most households kept pigs, chickens or goats, feeding them up on kitchen scraps, while suburban households might specialise in dairying or fattening up cattle (often reared far from the city due to their ability to walk themselves to market) on spent brewers' grain. The one exception to all this was grain, which could neither be grown in the city nor easily transported there, being heavy and bulky in relation to its value. For this reason, most pre-industrial cities remained small: in 1800, just 3% of the global population lived in settlements of 5,000 or more.[4]

Such dependence on grain gave maritime cities a decisive advantage over their land-locked neighbours, since their ability to import food from overseas allowed them to grow to a far greater size.[5] Rome famously pioneered this approach, conquering the neighbouring territories of Sicily, Sardinia and North Africa in order to extract grain from them in the form of tax. With an astonishing one million citizens at the height of its empire, the city imported grain, oil, wine, ham, honey and a fermented fish sauce called *liquamen* from across the Mediterranean, Black Sea and North Atlantic coasts.

The world's first metropolis, Rome, pioneered the extractive practices that feed modern cities today, removing nutrients from distant lands, never to be replaced. With its citizens craving increasingly exotic fare, local farmers concentrated on producing luxury foods such as fruit, vegetables, poultry, game and specialist delicacies such as pond fish and nut-stuffed dormice, while the city's remote hinterlands became gradually depleted, eventually failing altogether.

Two millennia on, it's not hard to see parallels between Rome's food culture and our own. The first city to fully outgrow its local hinterland, Rome demonstrated what I have called the urban paradox: the fact that, although those of us who live in cities think of ourselves as urban, in a deeper sense, we still dwell on the land. As Aristotle observed, we are 'political animals' who need society *and* nature in order to thrive. This duality lies at the heart of our modern dilemma: the more we gather together in cities, the further we get, both physically and mentally, from our sources of sustenance.

Lessons from Letchworth

Plato and Aristotle both argued that cities should remain small in order to foster a strong sense of community and render them self-sufficient – ideas that have permeated utopian thought ever since. Indeed, two of the most influential utopian tracts – Thomas More's 1516 *Utopia* and Ebenezer Howard's 1902 *Garden Cities of To-Morrow* – are clear descendants of the Greek ideal, arguing, as they do, for a return to the city-state.

More's *Utopia* – a thinly veiled critique of the power and greed of Tudor London – describes an imaginary kingdom of independent city-states, arranged a day's walk from one another. Utopians live in large urban blocks with generous back gardens, in which they grow beautiful fruit and vegetables.[6] Children are taught to grow things from a young age, and all citizens take turns in the fields, spending a mandatory two years there. Those who enjoy farming (which everyone does) can do it permanently if they choose. All land and property are held in common, and families and neighbourhoods share regular communal meals, which adults and children cook and eat together.

Utopia is notable for its concern with food, which is, however, never stated explicitly. The same could be said for Howard's garden city, which is essentially More's *Utopia* replayed for the railway age. Recognising our human need for both society and nature, Howard dubbed his garden city a 'Town-Country Magnet', arguing that a network of cities of limited size (with a maximum of 32,000 residents) surrounded by countryside could provide the benefits of urban and rural living, while negating the downsides of each.[7] Crucially, all the land occupied by the garden city was to be collectively owned by its residents in the form of a public trust, so that when values rose as a result of the city's presence, it would be citizens, not private landowners, who would benefit. Howard got this idea from the US economist Henry George, who argued in his influential 1879 book *Progress and Poverty* that all land should be considered to be publicly owned, and that anyone who wished to have exclusive use of it should pay a community land rent, or land value tax, for the privilege. Such a tax would not only help to fund public services, Howard believed, but would crucially help to preserve the agricultural land around the garden city, which private owners might otherwise be tempted to develop.

In 1903, Howard got the chance to realise his dream, when a group of leading industrialists backed him to build a prototype garden city in the village of Letchworth, Hertfordshire, 34 miles north of London. All

Frontispiece of Thomas More's *Utopia*, 1516. More's vision of an imaginary island with a network of closely connected city-states had its basis in the Greek ideal of *oikonomia*

and country.

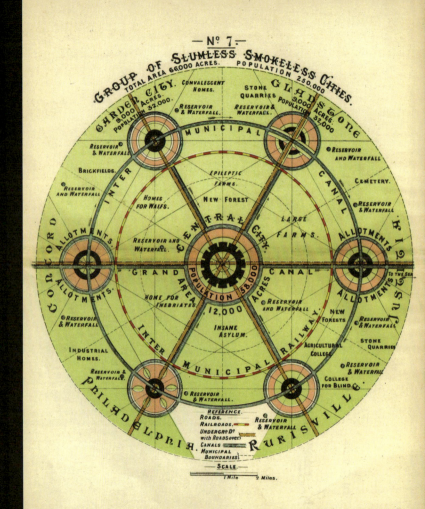

went well at first, and top architects Parker and Unwin were hired to draw up a masterplan reflecting Howard's vision. But the project struggled to attract investors at the low rates of return on offer, leading Howard's backers to renege on their promise to cede rents to the city, and prompting Howard to resign from the board.

Although Letchworth failed to fulfil Howard's vision, it nevertheless represents a milestone in urban planning, boasting a strong community trust and possession of the world's first protected 'green belt'. Yet the garden city model ultimately failed because it didn't score highly enough on the bottom line: *oikonomia* was trumped by *chrematistike*. One lesson from Letchworth is therefore this: sustainable food systems and communities are at odds with capitalist logic. If we want to build such systems and societies, therefore, it follows that we're going to need a different kind of economy.

Et in sitopia ego
As our most precious shared resource, food can form the basis of such an economy. By valuing food, we not only value the natural world whence it came, but those who produce it – who also need to eat. Unlike free market capitalism, which treats nature as expendable and strips the human out of every productive process, a sitopian economy would value the natural world and human endeavour above all else – and seek to balance the two. By aiming for a future in which everyone eats well, we can build a good life structured around our deepest shared needs and pleasures; a model whose internal logic leads naturally towards fairer societies more in balance with nature. By valuing food, in short, we can turn the vicious cycle of our capitalist economy into a virtuous one.

Since most food comes from the land where we also eat and live, it follows that in order to flourish, we need to share the land more equitably. This, in essence, is what Howard sought to do with a land value tax: give everyone access to society and nature, in order that they could flourish. A sitopian landscape would essentially do the same, which is to say, it would connect people to nature and one another through the growing, transporting, trading, cooking, sharing and recycling of food, and, above all, its enjoyment and celebration.

How might the world change if we were to attempt such a transformation? Instead of building ever-greater megacities and increasing the distance between ourselves and nature, we would surround our cities with regenerative farms and orchards, convert underused spaces such as rooftops, car parks and verges into allotments and orchards, and design adaptable homes and workplaces with large kitchens, shared gardens and balconies. Urban neighbourhoods would have allotments, community gardens and pocket farms, while rural areas would be repopulated and provided with essential services such as broadband, public transport, hospitals and schools. We would create millions of worthwhile jobs, and domestic life in both city and country would become far richer, as people spent more time growing, trading, cooking and sharing meals with families, friends and neighbours. New food hubs would rejuvenate city centres, while networks of small producers and suppliers would thrive, reconnecting cities with their hinterlands. Industrial feedlots and damaging 'Big Ag' would be replaced by smaller, mixed organic farms prioritising soil health, biodiversity, and carbon and water capture, with cattle raised on natural grassland or as part of regenerative farming systems. The food system would morph from its current dehumanised, exploitative state into something socially and ecologically regenerative.

Below: Ben Flanner, Brooklyn Grange Rooftop Farm, Brooklyn. A pioneer of urban rooftop farming, Flanner was the first person to gain planning permission to return industrial to agricultural use in New York City, sparking a movement that has since spread across the world.

Sitopia: A Landscape for Human and Non-Human Flourishing

MVRDV, masterplan for Almere Oosterwold. Built on reclaimed polderland, this masterplan for the expansion of the Dutch city of Almere incorporates farms and local food networks and is thus a modern example of an attempt to build sitopia.

70   Working at the Intersection: Architecture After the Anthropocene

If this all sounds a tad utopian, it is because, wherever food is valued, sitopia tends towards utopia. Yet such transformations are far from fantasy; on the contrary, they are already happening. The Food Movement is an international assembly of farmers, producers, groups and organisations who recognise the transformative power of food that is, in the words of Slow Food founder Carlo Petrini, 'good, clean and fair'.[8] Countless networks and projects, from community gardens, box schemes, farmers' markets and CSAs (Community Supported Agriculture farms), to international networks such as Slow Food, Transition Towns, the Milan Food Pact and Via Campesina, are using food's power to build a better, greener future. Meanwhile, architects and planners seek to reconnect city and country with projects such as MVRDV's food-based masterplan for Almere Oosterwold in the Netherlands, or Viljoen and Bohn's CPULs (Continuous Productive Urban Landscapes), which create fertile corridors through cities and out to the countryside.[9] Regenerative agriculture is also gaining traction, with projects such as Knepp Castle Estate in the UK, where longhorn cattle, red deer and Tamworth pigs roam in a rich habitat thronging with wildlife, showing that productivity and biodiversity can and do co-exist.[10]

We have all the knowledge and technology we need to a build a good sitopia; all we need now is the political vision. Covid could help us here, since it has shown so clearly what was wrong with our previous way of life and how we might start to fix it. For many able to work from home in the industrial world, for example, lockdown has been something of a revelation, as people have enjoyed spending more time with their families, observing the coming of spring in their local park, cooking and eating together or sharing food with neighbours. Of those interviewed in one UK survey, 42% said they valued food more as a result of lockdown, and just 9% said they wanted life to go back to the way it was before the pandemic.[11]

Covid's greatest legacy may be that it reminds us of what really makes us happy: a decent job, a nice home, spending time with family and friends, a supportive social network, closeness to nature. Simple things, in other words, that by readjusting our values, we can provide for everyone. While food is far from the only thing that matters in life, it is the only one that connects all the rest – which is what makes it such a potent medium of transformation. Sitopia will never be utopia – that, indeed, is its point – yet by learning to harness food's power to shape our lives for good, we can come close to the utopian dream of creating landscapes for human and non-human flourishing. As well as being the great connector, food is also a great leveller: the most potent symbol, apart from the Earth itself, of our commonality.

1. Megan Brenan, '40% of Americans believe in Creationism', Gallup, 26 July 2019, https://news.gallup.com/poll/261680/americans-believe-creationism.aspx.
2. See Carolyn Steel, *Sitopia: How Food Can Save the World*, London, Chatto & Windus, 2020.
3. See Aristotle, *The Politics*, trans. T A Sinclair, London, Penguin, 1981, p85.
4. Estimates by Philip M Hauser, quoted in Norbert Schoenauer, *6000 Years of Housing*, New York, W W Norton, 2000, p96.
5. Neville Morley estimates that it was 42 times cheaper to transport food over sea than over land in the ancient world. See Neville Morley, *Metropolis and Hinterland*, Cambridge, Cambridge University Press, 1996, p65.
6. Thomas More, *Utopia*, (1516), trans. Paul Turner, Penguin, 2003, p53.
7. Ebenezer Howard, *Garden Cities of To-Morrow*, (1902), Cambridge, MA, MIT Press Paperback Edition, 1965.
8. See Carlo Petrini, *Slow Food Nation: Why Our Food should be Good, Clean and Fair*, New York, Rizzoli, 2007, pp93–143.
9. See https://www.mvrdv.nl/projects/32/almere-oosterwold and Jorge Peña Díaz and Phil Harris, 'Urban agriculture in Havana, opportunities for the future', in André Viljoen, ed., *CPULs, Continuous Productive Urban Landscapes*, London, Architectural Press, 2005.
10. See Isabella Tree, *Wilding: The Return of Nature to a British Farm*, London, Picador, 2018.
11. Sue Pritchard, 'Finding the road to renewal', RSA blog, 17 April 2020, https://www.thersa.org/discover/publications-and-articles/rsa-blogs/2020/04/finding-the-road-to-renewal.

Cave_bureau, the Anthropocene Museum, AM 4.0, 2017–19. Nayece of the Turkana People.

PROFILE:
A Troublesome Trail of Improvision Towards the Chthulucene
Kabage Karanja and Stella Mutegi
The Anthropocene Museum

'The world is usually organized according to principles that flatter the dominant imagination'[1] Lesley Lokko

Very few geological terms have aroused such debate and critique as the Anthropocene – a word derived from the Greek word ánthrōpos, meaning 'human being', and cene meaning 'new' or 'recent', fused to describe the age of the human being. Periods in our relatively recent history have been instrumental in defining this age; in particular, the imperialist and colonial eras that spanned from the late eighteenth century right into the mid-twentieth century in succession. Periods where many indigenous peoples were exploited by an elitist few, spurred on through industrialisation and further still into modern and post-modern times of exponential demographic, economic and technological growth. It is incumbent on us to reflect that these periods coincided with the emergence of theories and movements of resistance against the imperial and colonial powers of our age, manifesting in many ways – from within the seats of power, but more so from outside, where a groundswell of freedom fighting groups emerged across the planet to directly confront this dark age, catapulted into being by a few white men.

Yet the term Anthropocene wasn't coined until the year 2000 by Nobel Laureate Paul J. Crutzen, and later built upon by scientists such as Jan Zalasiewicz, Jaia Syvitsky, Mark Williams and Naomi Oreskes, as well as many others via the Anthropocene Working Group (AWG) of the Subcommission on Quaternary Stratigraphy (SQS) in 2009[2] – stratigraphy is the branch of geology that studies rock layers, and the SQS is the constituent body that falls under the main International Commission on Stratigraphy, and subject to the International Union of Geological Sciences. So, it is under this hierarchical stratum that the Anthropocene Working Group has tasked itself to formally determine and present the merit of the Anthropocene as a potential new unit of geological time on the International Chronostratigraphic Chart.[3]

This proposed new age has naturally been challenged by many thinkers and provocateurs, who have established other labels such as the Plantationocene and Capitalocene. Of particular interest to this paper are the writings of Anna Tsing and Donna Haraway, who challenge the dominant imagination of the times we currently live in. Donna Haraway has said 'I along with others think the Anthropocene is more a boundary event than an epoch, like the K-Pg boundary between the Cretaceous and the Paleogene. The Anthropocene marks severe discontinuities; what comes after will not be like what came before. I think our job is to make the Anthropocene as short/thin as possible and to cultivate with each other in every way imaginable epochs to come that can replenish refuge.'[4] This is an epoch in the making, which Haraway calls the Chthulucene, embodying the past,

Cave_bureau, the Anthropocene Museum, AM 1.0, 2017–19. Bronze model of the Mau Mau Mbai Cave.

Left: Cave_bureau, the Anthropocene Museum, AM 4.0, 2017–19. Beaked whales of the Great Rift Valley.

Below: Cave_bureau, the Anthropocene Museum, AM 4.0, 2017–19. Origin is forever.

present and times to come, and representing a more positive and inclusive perspective on the future. Haraway also speaks of dynamic ongoing sym-chthonic forces and powers – of which people are a part – within which our collective ongoingness, as Haraway describes it, is profoundly at stake. She adds that '[o]ne way to live and die well as mortal critters in the Chthulucene is to join forces to reconstitute refuges, to make possible partial and robust biological-cultural-politicaltechnological recuperation and recomposition, which must include mourning irreversible losses'.[5]

This framing resonates with our own research at Cave_bureau as an enactment of what we call the Anthropocene Museum – a site of enquiry and space intended to confront the dominant western conception of our times. The Anthropocene Museum reframes this epoch through an African perspective in and through praxis. We retain the word 'Anthropocene' in its perturbing nature, and conjoin it with 'Museum' – a troubled institution in the colonial and post-colonial sense: 'We call them museums, but that's a euphemism, it might be better to call them warehouses of stolen loot. In 1897, British forces entered the Kingdom of Benin, modern-day Nigeria, and violently looted hundreds of priceless possessions; many are now on display in western museums and private collections.'[6]

The Anthropocene Museum is postulated on a planetary scale and as a marker in time, contemplating and confronting the conditions of our epoch – a period that follows a long history of the

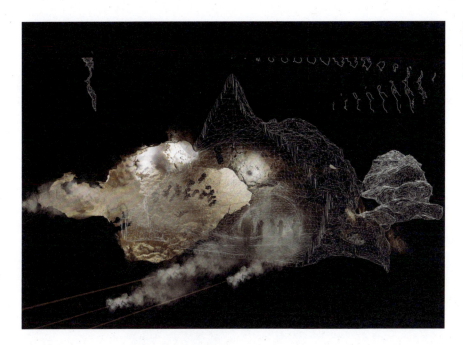

Cave_bureau, the Anthropocene Museum, AM 1.0, 2017–19. Mbai Cave, of geothermal steam and struggle.

enslavement and exploitation of non-European indigenous peoples. Amitav Ghosh in his book *The Great Derangement, Climate Change and the Unthinkable*, argues that western violence was vital in the formation of the world today.[7]

We set the context of the Anthropocene Museum at a time in the mid-twentieth century when the widespread formation and establishment of many liberating, anti-colonial grassroots movements across the planet took place and still continue. It is a time when much of this resistance found refuge in 'natural' environments, as was the case for the Mau Mau freedom fighters in colonial Kenya, who escaped into caves and forests, from where they staged their resistance. As children of parents who grew up in Kenya at that time, we reflect on the words of Donna Haraway about the mourning of irreversible losses, that stretch even further back to those of our ancestors sold to slavery in the seventeenth and eighteenth centuries. These losses continued more recently in the middle of the twenteith century, at the height of modernity, in ways that reprised the dehumanisation of wretched colonial times. This was a period when crimes against humanity were committed across the world by many European governments – in particular the British government – that continued even after the end of the Second World War.[8] Throughout this time our finite resources were stolen, and indeed continue to be taken away for the least amount of value possible, only to be resold back to us at the highest possible price.

PROFILE: The Anthropocene Museum: A Troublesome Trail of Improvision Towards the Chthulucene

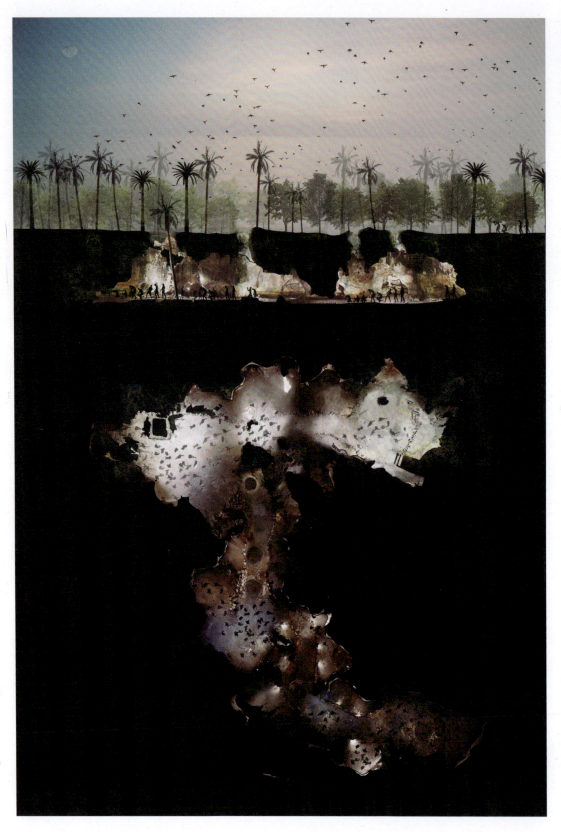

Opposite: Cave_bureau, the Anthropocene Museum, AM 1.0, 2017–19. Cave drawing analysing Mount Suswa's baboon parliament in Kenya, preceding Rome's Pantheon in Italy by over a million years.

Left: Cave_bureau, the Anthropocene Museum, AM 2.0, 2017–19. Shimoni Slave Cave cross-section and plan.

Cave_bureau, the Anthropocene Museum, AM 3.0, 2017–19. Venice Biennale, obsidian rain drawing.

PROFILE: The Anthropocene Museum: A Troublesome Trail of Improvision Towards the Chthulucene

In the midst of such great and continuous loss, we reflect on the liberating and cerebral spaces of refuge that our freedom-fighting forebears inhabited; in particular, caves. These were spaces where they contemplated how to defend their existence and to define an African – indeed a new human – state of the future. These primordial spaces of unrecognised architectural heritage, from an academic and practice-based standpoint, are engrained in our prehistoric consciousness. Remaining open to use, these spaces frame our understanding of the world moving forward, and offer a place from which to collectively reconstitute our existence as humans and non-humans together.

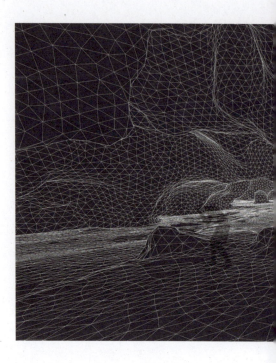

We choose to frame this discursive practice as a canon – a cave canon for that matter – stretching the history of architecture beyond the human life span. It is, for us at least, a powerful safe space where disregarded territories of architectural exploration such as race and 'identity' can become fully operational in architectural discourse and practice – territories that Lesley Lokko highlights in her book *White Papers Black Marks* – a book serendipitously published in the same year the Anthropocene was coined.[9] For indeed our world is organised according to principles that flatter the dominant imagination, but at what expense and for how long? To address this, we choose to take an epistemological and ontological journey that builds upon the

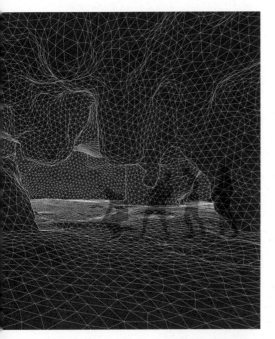

Above: Cave_bureau, the Anthropocene Museum, AM 2.0, 2017–19. Shimoni Slave Cave interior.

Opposite: Cave_bureau, the Anthropocene Museum, AM 3.0, 2017–19. Venice Biennale, obsidian rain installation.

Chthulucene's own inclusive rubric, reframing it through an improvised lens, which for us, in its quintessentially spiritual dimension, has a deeply African slant.

The improvisor, in repeating the work of ancestral models, is not replicating the past but affirming its potential ... the moment of vision and moment of harkening are the deep spaces of improvisation for the transformation of creative works.[10]

Welcome to the Anthropocene Museum, whose operations are spread across the planet. To date we have four main curated programmes on three continents – although modest, we believe they will collectively and cumulatively remain over time, the necessary ingredients to concertedly thin and shorten the Anthropocene as we know it, allowing for the emergence of a new and better epoch to come into being.

AM 1.0 in Mount Suswa and the Mbai Caves, exhibited in the Cooper Hewitt, Smithsonian Design Museum and the Cube Museum, Kerkrade, Netherlands in 2019.

AM 2.0 in the Shimoni Slave Caves along the Indian Ocean coast. Exhibited at the World Around Summit, online and in residence at the Solomon R. Guggenheim Museum in New York City, 2021.

AM 3.0 at the 17th International Architectural Exhibition, Venice Biennale, How will we live together?

AM 4.0 at the Cave Canon at the Cascades exhibition at the Museum of Art, Architecture and Technology (MAAT) in Lisbon.

In these four locations are both physical and digital manifestations, set in motion as a continuum of discursive, existential exhibitions with local community groups who are engaged in practices of resistance. Our programmes bring the subject of these resistive practices to light using film, drawing, writing and the construction of systems that transcend the self-obsessed bricks-and-mortar practice of architecture for architecture's sake. We call this a 'reverse architecture', where through the use of laser scanning technology of specific community-run caves, we produce 'conventional' architectural drawings to curate our 'baraza', which in Swahili refers to open dialogue. We believe that over time these exhibitions have the capacity to begin the 'thinning-out' process of the Anthropocene and, we hope, imagine and pray, gradually metamorphosise beyond the yet-unseen confines of the Chthulucene. The Anthropocene Museum in this regard remains operational and continuously open until the ravages induced by our presence on Earth are suppressed, if not reversed. It goes without saying that the current state of architectural thought and practice in this regard remains primarily complicit and an impediment to the ongoing cause.

1 Lesley Naa Norle Lokko, *White Papers Black Marks: Architecture, Race Culture*, Minneapolis, University of Minnesota Press, p33.
2 Edward Burtynsky, et al., *Anthropocene*, Göttingen, Steidl, 2018, p36.
3 Ibid.
4 Donna Haraway, 'Anthropocene, Capitalocene, Plantationocene, Chthulucene: Making kin', *Environmental Humanities*, vol. 6, 2015, p160.
5 Ibid.
6 Zing Tsjeng, 'Empires of dirt: Why some museums are filled with stolen objects', https://www.youtube.com/watch?v=vfCHdIbtNC0.
7 Amitav Ghosh, *The Great Derangement*, Chicago, University of Chicago Press, 2016, p80.
8 Caroline Elkins, *Britain's Gulag*, Oxford, Bodley Head, 2014, pp153, 194.
9 Lokko, *White Papers Black Marks: Architecture, Race, Culture*.
10 Araya Asgedom, 'The unsounded space' in Lokko, *White Papers Black Marks*, p258.

PROFILE: The Anthropocene Museum: A Troublesome Trail of Improvisation Towards the Chthulucene

Ensamble Studio, Ca'n Terra, 2018–20. A slice of rock has been cut from the ceiling to create a skylight. Where it has fallen, a secret garden has been made, allowing a tree to grow in the interior space.

PROFILE:
For Landscapes of the Post-Anthropocene
Antón García-Abril and Débora Mesa
Ca'n Terra

Ca'n Terra reads as *House of the Earth*, the Earth being both site and owner. Three years ago, Ca'n Terra had no name, much less a meaning. It was just an oversized hole in the ground, an inconvenient consequence that is easier to disregard than face. Yet another expression of an era – the Anthropocene – that has largely proven the power of humans to reshape our planet. And it is not alone; currently there are numerous catalogued *pedreras* (quarries) on the Balearic island of Menorca; only a fraction are active or protected, while many have quickly shifted from resource to dump.

The quarrying of Mares stone has been an activity inherent to the development of the island that saw in its stony substrate the most accessible and robust material for construction. From the prehistoric monuments, settlements and caves of the Talaiotic society, to the small excavations that today make the basements of many rural houses, and the bigger and most recent quarries meant to feed the construction of urban developments, the land has historically served as resource, support and shelter.

Our encounter with Ca'n Terra can only be described as a moment of serendipity. It was not looking to be found and we were not looking to find it. Located in a non-touristic rural quarter and carved underground to optimise the surface area for ranching and agriculture, this abandoned quarry could easily pass unnoticed. And even if noticed, its state of abandonment and deterioration could scare away the most daring. The terrain was uneven; the yellowish stone covered with a thick black make-up of mould and dirt persistently stuck over decades, partially eroded and cracked; and inside, diverse animals toured, camped and lay fossilised. Traces of occupation suggest that during the Spanish Civil War, and more specifically the Battle of Menorca in 1939, this *pedrera* offered a dry shelter for militia

Ensamble Studio, Ca'n Terra, 2018–20. Exterior view of the terrain above the abandoned quarry.

and ammunition alike. A rusted Mercedes car, vestiges of electrical circuits, ventilation chimneys and a couple of guard houses testify to temporary use, or rather abuse. It fascinates us that such a place, even if unplanned and unwanted, could be squatted and later overlooked for almost a century.

The space that opens up before us is intriguing. From a distance it might seem like one more of the multiple natural cavities formed through the erosion of the calcareous rock that is characteristic of the island. But as we enter, we begin to identify steps, columns and stone slabs, which neither seem to follow Cartesian geometries nor to have been carved solely by the action of wind and water. Despite the absence of architectural logic, we cannot stop reading the space and the structures we start to appreciate as architecture – an architecture created inadvertently, by means of an excavation process with an industrial purpose, which paradoxally builds a space never intended to be inhabited, but whose scale, topology and materiality invite us to do so.

Like this place, there are countless others around the world – landscapes exploited for the construction of structures, often remote, and profoundly altered to enjoy a short, useful life, later passing into oblivion. As young architects, we spent many days working from sunrise to sunset in the Galician granite quarries. We approached them motivated by our ignorance in matters of stone and our desire to learn from the experts. The brutal excavation of the landscape captured by our senses in these industrial sites – the cuts, the explosions, the displacements that transform matter into material, and nature into artifice – are recorded in our consciousness and remind us, in each project, that every act of creation implies destruction. The design decisions we make as architects have local and global implications, and we are responsible for them whether we like it or not.

We did not witness the exploitation of Ca'n Terra, but when we found it, we detected the same automatism and lack of imagination, or anticipation, that we had seen before; the kind that turns valuable places into waste. Far from being discouraged by the responsibility of appropriating and intervening in the space, we are mobilised by the extraordinary opportunity for reinvention that we sense.

The entrance to this post-human space occurs through a slight descent and a progressive transition from daylight to the deepest darkness. Our vision does not manage to capture all the details, but it intuits them, and we use the most advanced laser scanning technology to register the space, and render its last wrinkle, releasing rays of light that, in their contact with the stone, transform real into virtual. The digitised information that we obtain as a point cloud allows us to analyse what exists and understand it before thinking about transforming it. The 3D model and the drawings that we extract from

Below: Ensamble Studio, Ca'n Terra, 2018–20. Interior view of the existing excavated space discovered by the architects.

Left: Ensamble Studio, Ca'n Terra, 2018–20. Exterior facade built with light membranes, which mask the functions of the interior spaces and impart a crepuscular atmosphere.

it are of an overwhelming beauty, and a precision that transcends the properties of the physical, revealing atmospheric qualities that belong to the realm of experience more so than of representation. The continuous negotiation between the power of the manual cutting tool and the heterogeneous consistency of the stone material results in broken lines, discontinuous planes and continuous changes of direction that are due to technical limitations, but that we allow ourselves to read as artistic freedoms. It is the act of discovery and interpretation that we understand in this project as the most creative, the one that triggers the process of imagining a new reality that is yet to be built. We were not the ones who carved the stone and, as a result, formed a space of such characteristics and proportions, with a freshness in its complexion that we admire especially for its randomness; but the simple fact of having found it moves us to give it a new meaning.

The project then starts from the identification of a valuable pre-existence. There is no room for a *tabula rasa* approach. The table is already set. The challenge is how to intervene in this powerful place, doing justice to what was there before we arrived. It is not the first time we have faced such difficulty: designing *Structures of Landscape* in the sublime geography of Tippet Rise was an exercise in measurement and imagination that had us, for three years, observing and conceiving a way of creating architectures that the land could recognise as its own. In the case of Ca'n Terra, the structure and the space were already in existence, so the scope of work was even less obvious.

Ensamble Studio, Ca'n Terra, 2018–20. A pool cut into the grotto is dressed with a minimal furnishing of lounge cushions.

84 Working at the Intersection: Architecture After the Anthropocene

We envision a collaboration across times, a process of layering that we recognise in many hybrid architectures that we admire. We have studied and walked with emotion through the Mosque of Córdoba and across the Ponte Vecchio (to mention two of a great many), undertaken the transformation of Madrid's Old Slaughterhouse into Casa del Lector, and without going too far from Ca'n Terra, in Lithica, effected the conversion of an industrial space into a cultural one. This long-term vision of architecture is grounded on the certainty that good architecture, like cities or wine, takes shape with time and accumulated experience. The interest in the hybrid, the ambiguous, the uncertain ... speaks of a form of innovation that makes the most of what it encounters, and elevates it, welcoming imperfection.

The sun and the Earth serve as our inexhaustible sources of energy, and we start with small actions that have a disproportionate impact. We remove the soil accumulated by the passage of time to recover the firm ground provided by the stone at different levels, and we relocate it in a way that protects the interior space from the run-off that floods the ex-quarry when the 'cold drop'[1] arrives. We clean the surfaces with pressurised water, returning the stone to its natural color and the space to its original luminosity. Without further artifice, our field of vision and action is thus expanded. Following the hands that excavated this space hundreds of years ago, ours resume its construction with intrinsic operations: cuts that provide

Ensamble Studio, Ca'n Terra, 2018–20. Light has been brought into the interior spaces through the use of translucent plastic sheeting.

PROFILE: Ca'n Terra: For Landscapes of the Post-Anthropocene 85 air and light to areas of permanent shadow. To sustain the habitability achieved, we protect the space with translucent membranes, as tense curtains that delimit without closing. Architecture appears and, consequently, the possibility of inhabitation. We leave the space flexible and indeterminate, so that objects and functions move, as do light, humidity and comfort conditions during the day and through the seasons. We are nomads in our own home. We do not seek the stability of the sealed interiors to which modernity has accustomed us. We intuit that another way of living on Earth is possible if we embrace the impermanence of the weather, optimise the consumption of resources, work with the most basic principles of architecture and free ourselves from many of the ties that limit our creativity as architects and our consciousness as human beings.

Ensamble Studio, Ca'n Terra, 2018–20. A crevice cut into the sandstone creates spaces to sit.

Ca'n Terra lives in nature and builds with it. Primary elements – air, light, earth and fire – are its construction materials. This work of architecture humanises an abandoned industrial site, noticing its existence and provisioning it solely with what is necessary to enable habitation without further exploitation. Unearthing, cleaning and carving define our design actions, and they are able to infuse life into a previously dormant place. Equal parts land, earthwork and home, Ca'n Terra offers a memorable space to reconcile human actions on the environment with those of nature, to learn to live and to build more lightly, to redefine what comfort is and how to achieve it with sensitivity. Our work here as architects, as clients and as users mixes, as mixed as the nature of this place, transcending unimaginative categorisations to open our eyes to new horizons.

Ensamble Studio, Ca'n Terra, 2018–20. The membranes continue through the interior spaces, opening up here as a threshold. This approach is seen as an act of learning to live and build more lightly.

1   The 'cold drop' (Spanish: *gota fría*) is an archaic meteorological term commonly used in Spain, which has come to refer to any high-impact rainfall events occurring in the autumn along the Spanish Mediterranean coast.

PROFILE: Ca'n Terra: For Landscapes of the Post-Anthropocene

PROFILE:
The Architecture of Analogous Habitats
Ariane Lourie Harrison
Pollinators Pavilion,
Hudson, NY, USA

The architecture of analogous habitats

The idea of the Anthropocene, a geological period named after the dominance of humans as the most significant evolutionary force on the planet, is neatly encapsulated in sustainable architecture's focus on one species: humans. An architecture for the post-Anthropocene could begin to engage any of the almost two million identified species on the planet. The challenge of constructing habitats for non-humans opens architecture to a broad terrain, engaging the biological, conservation and computer sciences. Harrison Atelier's Pollinators Pavilion seeks to provide an ecological analogue to native bees' historically preferred habitats. As an analogous habitat, the Pollinators Pavilion both replicates and integrates some of the physical conditions of historic habitats into its panellised construction; yet by integrating a monitoring system into the habitat, it prototypes a post-Anthropocenic view of architecture, extending intelligent accommodation to non-human species, and recognising the global urgency posed by biodiversity loss.

In founding Harrison Atelier, Seth and I asked ourselves, 'why would architecture be limited to designing for one species?' This question of how architecture can extend beyond its anthropocentric viewpoint prompted our initial design research in the form of performance, installations and writing. Our web of co-existence is described as biodiversity, whose logic, aside from an ethical regard for other life forms, also benefits humans in maintaining a reserve of resources and competitive balance among species. Building for other species is of course pragmatic given human dependence on other species' ecological services. In delving into this problem as architects, we encounter data gaps in our understanding of how to construct successful habitats. The Pollinators Pavilion demonstrates the benefits of deep collaboration between science, design and research communities in building an analogous habitat, and the role that this type of design can play in broadening climate literacy.

Opposite: Pollinators Pavilion at Old Mud Creek Farm, Hudson, NY, 2020 by Harrison Atelier. The form is intended to recall a spiky grain of pollen and a bee's bristling compound eye, highlighting the manner in which bringing a species into greater visibility may generate greater ethical regard.

Right: Panel, Pollinators Pavilion at Old Mud Creek Farm, Hudson, NY, 2020 by Harrison Atelier. A single panel seeks to embed different functions while allowing each surface to serve different species (bees' nesting tubes are accessible on one side, human technology on the other).

The Birds and The Bees, project drawing by Harrison Atelier. Early work on multiple species involved speculative drawing together of species, in this example by Matthew Bohne.

Habitats for whom?

It seems sadly fitting that the Anthropocene coincides with the sixth mass extinction of species. Species are being extinguished to a large degree because of habitat loss. If, according to the oft-cited statistic that by 2050, 68% of the human population will be living in cities, then we anticipate only further depletion of habitats for non-humans.[1]

Within this global framework of species loss, the decline of native and non-native pollinators today poses a major threat to the global agriculture food supply: 90% of the planet's 25,000 bee species are native bees, responsible for 75% of non-agricultural pollination globally. Global climate change (and intensive development) has amplified pollinator population decline so significantly that predictions of an 'insect apocalypse' appear regularly in the media.[2]

The term 'pollinator' tends to invoke the charismatic honeybee, whose social organisation, elaborate hives and honey-making dominate the anthropocentric understanding of bees. This popular view hardly considers the diversity of native bees, whose colour and size vary from blue orchard bees, to tiny sweat bees and furry, bumbling carpenter bees. The mason bee does the pollinating work of 100 honeybees, yet produces neither hive nor honey. The majority of native bees are considered 'solitary', that is, they lay eggs in burrows and tunnels underground. Cavity-dwelling solitary bees make discreet and opportunistic nests in abandoned burrows, holes and reeds: varied habitats that are hard to identify but easy to eradicate.[3]

Such elusive nesting habits contribute to the data gaps around native pollinators, including our understanding of some basic aspects of solitary bee biology, and species-level distributional and inhabitation patterns. Moreover, solitary bees are identified typically in a process called destructive sampling involving trapping, capture and killing the bee subject. Monitoring becomes a time-consuming and expensive prospect, and destructive sampling further reduces solitary bee populations. Can architecture, as an art of enclosure, contribute to monitoring? We could argue that designing any habitat for the diverse and declining insect species should engage the scientific need for monitoring and data collection, given that computer vision and deep learning, paired with cameras and sensors, can record species behaviours in an effective and non-invasive manner.[4]

A panel for pollinators

Designing habitation for non-humans invites architecture to consider surprising dimensions: native pollinators nest in spaces of 1cm in diameter and 10cm in depth, which accommodates three to six native bee egg cells. This tiny scale could comfortably fit into the exteriors of our buildings. The architectural cladding element of the panel offered a site for Harrison Atelier to focus on built work from the Species Wall in

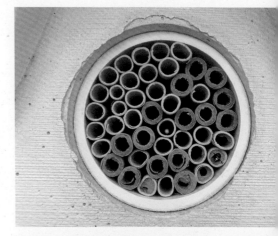

Top: Panel inhabited by bees, Pollinators Pavilion at Old Mud Creek Farm, Hudson, NY, 2020 by Harrison Atelier. A brief month on site demonstrated native bees and wasps using the nesting tubes.

Bottom: Back of panel, Pollinators Pavilion at Old Mud Creek Farm, Hudson, NY, 2020 by Harrison Atelier. The camera and motion sensors are connected to a microprocessor powered by a solar array on the top of the pavilion.

Clermont, NY to speculative projects such as The Birds and the Bees. The panel in these examples was cast from concrete, an inert material from a species perspective (although with a high carbon footprint from an ecological perspective), and its thickness accommodated spaces for other species to inhabit. We observed successful inhabitation of these panels in the Species Wall, but as architects were unable to suggest what was actually living in these spaces. We needed to develop panels with more intelligence: integrating cameras to provide long-term observation and produce photographic data to share with the scientific community capable of identifying these species.

So what does a pollinator nesting panel need to do? Provide shelter from the rain; accommodate sufficient depth for nesting; not off-gas or leach chemicals onto potential inhabitants; allow for nesting cleaning and maintenance; create sufficient 'viewing' space from a camera's perspective; protect microprocessors from rain; and ideally connect to an off-grid power source for the monitoring equipment function and data relay. The panel becomes a thick sandwich of interrelated functions. What essentially constitutes front-of-house includes insects' access to the exterior, while back-of-house addresses human access to monitoring equipment.

The concrete panel that we developed for the Pollinators Pavilion accommodates these functions with a conceptual structure of an 'S' curve: a single surface with a protrusion or cavity housing all the monitoring technology. Each panel contains a circular hole in which to lodge a bundle of 30 to 50 152mm-long nesting tubes of diameters from 3–9mm in cardboard, bamboo, paper, and wood. Initially intended as rain protection over the nesting tubes, the pointed canopies (or 'thorns') evolved in our work to house solar-powered monitoring equipment: motion sensors which, when triggered by insect movement, prompt an endoscopic camera to photograph the insect. Thus what is a rain canopy, seen from one side of the panel, becomes a housing for cameras, sensors and microprocessors. Prototypes of these panels developed at scale allowed us to work through power and connection issues and ultimately laid the successful groundwork for developing our award-winning cladding system for the Pollinators Pavilion.

New audiences for pollinators

Harrison Atelier designed and built the Pollinators Pavilion as a visitor centre and analogous habitat for native cavity-dwelling pollinating bees for Old Mud Creek Farm in Hudson, NY. The 2,500-acre organic farm is integrated with Hudson Carbon, an open-source research collaborative that quantifies the effects of regenerative agriculture on soil carbon sequestration. As a visitor centre, the Pollinators Pavilion seeks to raise awareness of the dynamic contribution of

Below: Species Wall, Clermont Historical Site, NY by Harrison Atelier. The twigs emerging from the aperture indicate a nest within the panel, while wasps' nests were made behind other panels as well.

PROFILE: Pollinators Pavilion: The Architecture of Analogous Habitats native pollinators to regenerative farming. Its design accommodates humans and pollinators: its domed form and spiky shape recall elements from the insect world, from the bristled compound eye to microscopic images of pollen. Its overall scale, as a grouping of 320 panels, approaches a megastructure from an insect perspective and is designed to amplify insect presence to humans. The lower registers of 124 panels contain nesting tubes, while the smaller panels admit light. An unrolled elevation becomes a grid or matrix for testing nesting preferences according to tube aperture sizes and materiality as well as orientation to the sun.

We became architects who do field studies. Starting in September 2020, we collected about 500 images per day, per camera (three pictures per minute for three hours per day). These field studies were planned to be extended to the full nesting season in 2021 over four months, producing an unlabelled database of just under one million images. The database is processed through a

Hempcrete Pollinators Pavilion rendering, Governors Island, NY by Harrison Atelier. This hempcrete version of the Pollinators Pavilion seeks to extend the research by creating hempcrete 'bee blocks' so that what is a human-scaled pavilion can be easily disassembled into bee-scaled distributed habitats.

Working at the Intersection: Architecture After the Anthropocene

View up inside Pollinators Pavilion at Old Mud Creek Farm, Hudson NY, 2020 by Harrison Atelier. The interior of the pavilion seeks to highlight the constructed nature of the analogous habitat that assembles Baroque motifs, nesting tubes from historic habitats and microprocessors.

machine-learning system (also of Harrison Atelier's design) designed to predict the family of native pollinating species without trapping and killing them. Machine learning and artificial intelligence become vital means of organising documentation of the non-human multitudes, whose loss would undermine entire food webs and ecosystems. We participate in the global efforts to automate pollinator identification, helping to fill in information on habitation patterns that lies outside of the scope of citizen-science applications such as iNaturalist. Insect identification lies well outside the purview of architecture. But designing an infrastructure for insect monitoring within a pavilion facade is less so, when architects accept that ecological design requires close collaboration with scientists. The next developments of the Pollinators Pavilion including a new site on Governors Island include digital platforms to translate datasets into apps and virtual experiences that can engage broader audiences in the appreciation of biodiversity. Another consideration involves disarticulating the scale of the pavilion into an aggregation of nesting building blocks. And a third consideration explores more sustainable types of concrete by introducing hempcrete for new panels.

Analogous habitats

In scientific parlance, analogous habitats refer to human-made artificial ecosystems that can support native biodiversity, in part due to material, structural and functional resemblance to natural ecosystems. In architecture, the term analogous resonates with the idea of uncanny formal kinships, charged by historical and repressed memory, *déjà vu* and projection, as articulated by Aldo Rossi.[5] We would suggest that these two meanings intertwine in the Pollinators Pavilion. Making insect habitation into a relatively monumental format brings the topic into human sight-lines. An architecture of analogous habitats amplifies non-human presences, bringing them into our ethical regard. An architecture of analogous habitats also requires new protocols of care: monitoring, maintaining, recording; its collaborative formats approach a new usage as an ecological infrastructure, becoming an agent of climate literacy in the post-Anthropocene.

1 Gerardo Ceballos, Paul R. Ehrlich and Peter H. Raven, 'Vertebrates on the brink as indicators of biological annihilation and the sixth mass extinction', *Proceedings of the National Academy of Sciences*, June 2020, vol. 117, no. 24, pp13596–13602; DOI: 10.1073/pnas.1922686117.
2 Brooke Jarvis, 'The insect apocalypse is here', *New York Times Magazine*, 27 November 2018, https://www.nytimes.com/2018/11/27/magazine/insect-apocalypse.html.
3 Bryan Danforth, Robert Minckley and John Neff, *The Solitary Bees: Biology, Evolution, Conservation*, Princeton, Princeton University Press, 2019.
4 Toke T Høye, et al., 'Deep learning and computer vision will transform entomology', *Proceedings of the National Academy of Sciences*, 12 January 2021, pp108–18, e2002545117, https://doi.org/10.1073/pnas.2002545117.
5 Daniel Sherer, *The Architecture and Art of the Analogous City*, Princeton University School of Architecture exhibition, 2018.

Alexandra Daisy Ginsberg, *The Wilding of Mars*, 2019. Installation view of *The Wilding of Mars* at What If ... On Utopia in Art, Architecture and Design, Neues Museum, Nuremberg, Germany, 2020.

CASE STUDY:
The Wilding of Mars

Alexandra Daisy Ginsberg

Human dreams of colonisation are not limited to Earth. We see Mars, untouched by Earth life, as barren, treacherous, beautiful; another planet to colonise. But humans invariably become exploiters. Instead, could we imagine Mars colonised only by plants, flourishing without us? *The Wilding of Mars* is an immersive video and sound artwork by the author, which simulates the growth of a planetary wilderness, seeded with Earth life forms. In exhibition, a wild garden on Mars thrives over millennia, its growth visible over human hours.

The aim is not to terraform Mars; here the planet is simply a repository for the mechanism of life. Plant life takes Mars in a different direction and Mars may take life elsewhere. In the installation, two simulations run in parallel; endless possible worlds emerge, inviting the viewer to question the assumption that space colonisation must be for human benefit. There are other paths life could take. Might leaving the planet to other life forms be the ultimate unnatural act for humans? Can we imagine Mars except as a place for ourselves?

The violent history of colonisation and the traumas repeatedly inflicted on peoples, species and our shared environment seem to be forgotten amidst the techno-utopian promises of the new billionaire colonialists selling us Mars. They describe a new, unexplored frontier for exploitation; a *tabula rasa* for humanity (or

Alexandra Daisy Ginsberg, *The Wilding of Mars*, 2019. Landscape 2: Year 895,788 (simulation screenshot).

Above Clockwise: Alexandra Daisy Ginsberg, *The Wilding of Mars*, 2019. Plant Cam 2, Landscape 2: Year 640,000 (simulation screenshot).

Alexandra Daisy Ginsberg, *The Wilding of Mars*, 2019. Plant Cam 3, Landscape 1: Year 235,000 (simulation screenshot).

Alexandra Daisy Ginsberg, *The Wilding of Mars*, 2019. Simulation 1, Landscape 1: Year 573,211 (simulation screenshot).

Alexandra Daisy Ginsberg, *The Wilding of Mars*, 2019. Simulation 2, Landscape 1: Year 573,211 (simulation screenshot).

for a few members of it) to exploit; a place to emancipate humans from the nature we have evolved alongside. Whether we have the right to colonise another planet and its supposedly empty frontiers – and whether indigenous life exists or not – is ignored.

The Wilding of Mars is an artwork that questions this utopian narrative. A multi-screen video and sound installation simulates the growth of a planetary wilderness seeded with Earth life forms. In this alternative world, Mars is colonised only by plants, flourishing without us. Can we imagine humans not as exploiters, but protectors of other species?

Three rows of paired screens show a wild garden on Mars thriving over a million years, its growth visible in a human hour. The pioneers are seeded in stages as conditions become more tolerable. We watch the plants invade northwards from the South Pole, creeping up the rows as time passes. Each vista is set up in the style of colonial landscape painting.

The pioneer species chosen are extremophiles: organisms that thrive in the harshest conditions on Earth, which are somewhat closer to Mars's brutal climate. These beings are wind-pollinated, eliminating the need for other lifeforms to be introduced. The pioneers slowly build an ecosystem under Martian conditions. To create this ecological and evolutionary simulation, every lichen, algae and plant pioneer is assigned a range of values for three parameters based on their Earth needs: water, temperature and nutrients (combining soil and air). As more water is released from the melting Martian ice-cap, more water-hungry species can thrive.

CASE STUDY: The Wilding of Mars

As plants populate the planet, each adds nutrients to the soil and thickens the atmosphere, warming the planet and allowing the less hardy species to appear.

The aim however is not to terraform Mars; here it is simply a repository for the mechanism of life. We watch strange new plant forms emerge with darker leaves to acclimatise to Mars's reduced atmospheric UV protection. Plant life takes Mars in a different direction, and Mars may take life elsewhere.

These new subspecies are the descendants of their pioneering ancestors. For example, the strange *Saxifraga oppositifolia martia* subsp. *sim-1-035* originates from *Saxifraga oppositifolia*, the purple saxifrage. Reflecting the scientific tradition on Earth that incites us to name things to know them, each descendent is named, documented and entered into a database. Adding the suffix of Mars (*martia*) extends Earth's Linnean binomial naming convention, devised to catalogue life as we know it. The fact that these subspecies do not actually exist is simply acknowledged in the prefix of 'sim' before their subspecies barcode.

The Wilding of Mars prioritises a non-human perspective. Humans are the alien viewers of a wilderness that we can only explore digitally and from a distance. With a million years passing in an hour, each pair of screens allows us to watch life in plant

Alexandra Daisy Ginsberg, *The Wilding of Mars*, 2019. Pioneers and Descendants: seeded and generated species from Simulation 1.

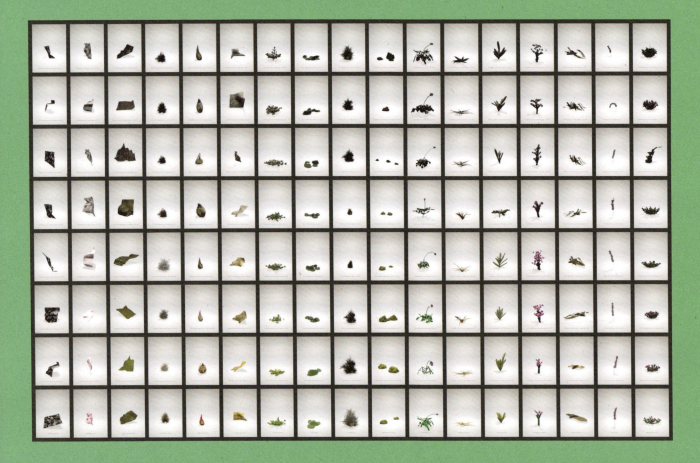

100   Working at the Intersection: Architecture After the Anthropocene

Detail of Alexandra Daisy Ginsberg's, *The Wilding of Mars*, 2019. Pioneers and Descendants: seeded and generated species from Simulation 1.

time, confronting the modern view of plants as static beings. In each row, the left-hand screen allows us to perceive plants colonising the landscape, while the right-hand screen zooms in on more intimate moments from those scenes, where we can watch plants as they visibly swell and blossom. The generative soundscape imagines their cells creaking as they multiply, set against the background atmosphere. The volume increases as the Martian atmosphere thickens and sound travels further. Voyeuristic camera angles heighten the sense of human intrusion. At the bottom of each screen, we see the most explicit evidence of the human gaze. An information bar logs the year, camera view, conditions, population, new subspecies evolved and those gone extinct.

The Wilding of Mars is not a proposal for alternatives to humanity's colonisation of Mars, nor a proposition for a back-up planet for lifeforms threatened on Earth. Two simulations run in parallel in the installation: a second set of six screens shows a different version of the same process. Two different possible worlds emerge to be compared and evaluated, with different lifeforms and atmospheric conditions and events. Watching a meadow juxtaposed against a fierce thousand-year sandstorm, the assumption that space colonisation is our destiny or even a human right seems flimsy. There are many other paths life could take. Might leaving the planet to other lifeforms be the ultimate unnatural act for humans? Can we imagine Mars except as a place for ourselves?

The Wilding of Mars, like all colonial endeavours, is still a violent act. We may see no humans, but this is just colonisation-by-proxy. Mars is inescapably transformed into another world. But it is transformed into a place to reflect back towards Earth. The planetary perspective can be useful to see the limits of our imagination. Mars is no longer a utopia, but a heterotopia: a place that is not better or worse, but different. It is another world from which we can observe and challenge our own nature.

Credits
Research and development: Dr Alexandra Daisy Ginsberg, Ness Lafoy, Johanna Just, Iona Mann, Stacie Woolsey
Software development: Tom Betts/Nullpointer, Jelena Viskovic, Ana Maria Nicolaescu
Sound: Sam Conran
With thanks to: Professor Luis Campos, Baruch S. Blumberg NASA/Library of Congress Chair in Astrobiology 2016–17; Dr Lynn Rothschild, NASA; Professor James Head, Brown University, Lisa White
With support from: Cité du Design, Saint-Étienne
Commissioned by: Vitra Design Museum, The Design Museum

CASE STUDY:
Bat Cloud, Buffalo, NY, USA

Joyce Hwang

Opposite: Ants of the Prairie, Bat Cloud, June 2012. Buffalo, NY. From afar, the hanging vessels designed for bat habitation appear like a cloud, hovering in the trees.

Below: Ants of the Prairie, Bat Cloud, 2012. Plan diagram of Bat Cloud installation in Tifft Nature Preserve, Buffalo, NY.

Bat Cloud is an urban intervention, initially conceived of as both a functioning bat habitat and a device to draw public awareness to bats as a critical part of our ecosystem. The installation comes into view as a shimmering mass, hovering between the trees. From afar, the piece appears as a silver-coloured cloud. Viewed from a closer range, the individual units within the cloud – or 'pods' as we were calling them – become discernible within the cluster.

Our research team, in consultation with biologists, developed the design of the prototypical 'pod' to support bat habitation in various ways, specifically considering bat species in New York State, such as the little brown bat and big brown bat. Spatially, the uppermost part of the pod is subdivided into several thin cavities, providing thin crevice-like roost spaces, of approximately 5cm long by 35cm wide by 2cm deep, a spatial volume that reflects recommendations for constructing standard bat houses. Materially, the pods are built from thermally insulating layers, including air-filled bubble wrap and heat-reflecting thermal 'blanket' sheets. In response to bats' needs for warm thermal environments, the reflective metallic sheet performs similarly to an

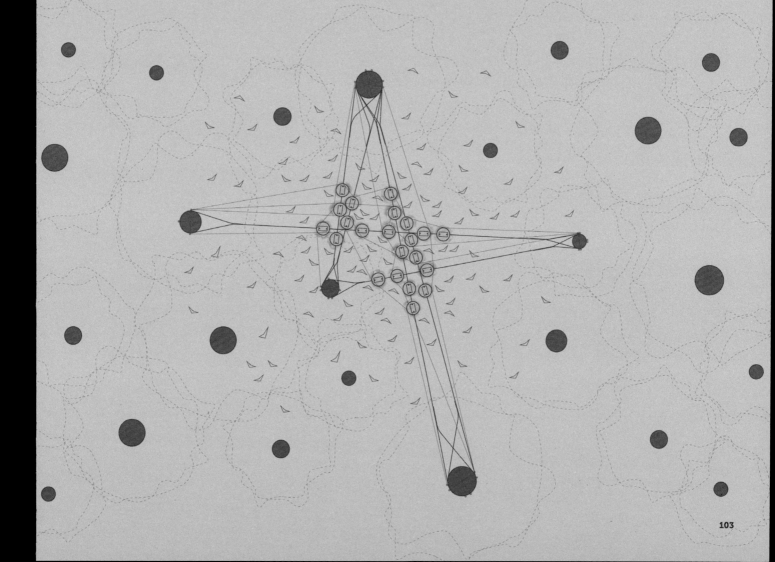

'emergency blanket,' or a reflective covering that one might wear after a long-distance run, to capture body heat. The hypothesis is that if the pods were occupied, the bats' warm-blooded body heat could be reflected back into the roosting chambers, to maintain their 'interior' environments at suitably warm temperatures.

Bat Cloud is located in Tifft Nature Preserve, a 265-acre area of restored habitat and trails in South Buffalo. The site was used as a municipal landfill in the 1950s and 1960s; later in the 1970s, it was capped with clay and soil, and began its transformation into a nature preserve. Due to its condition as a capped landfill, we were given the restriction to not install an in-ground foundation in order not to disrupt the cap. Our solution for structuring the project, therefore, was to utilise five existing eastern cottonwood trees on site as structural anchors to support stainless-steel wire rope cables. To prevent stripping of tree bark, the cables were wrapped in rubber sleeves where they came into contact with the tree trunks. These cables serve as the primary structure upon which the bat pods are hung. The structure of each pod was formed using a layer of stainless-steel wire mesh, folded into shape and bolted together. All together, the stainless-steel cables and pod structures, as well as the stainless-steel bolting and hanging hardware, were specified to resist the weathering effects of snowy winters and the intense winter weather near the Buffalo waterfront in particular.

Installed in 2012, Bat Cloud was designed initially as part of Fluid Culture, an event series by the University at Buffalo Humanities Institute organised by Colleen Culleton and Justin Read, both UB professors in the Department of Romance Languages and Literatures. Reflecting on the year-long series' intent to bring together artists and scholars in conversation about water, globalisation and culture, we focused the design of Bat Cloud not only on habitat and structural considerations, but also on how it might be 'read' and included in public discourse. As such, the project begins to address questions about the invisibility of – and even disdain towards – bats in our public consciousness, despite their role as a critical part of our ecosystem, as pollinators and a 'natural pesticide' for mosquitoes. In contrast to more typical bat houses that often fade into the background, Bat Cloud was designed to stand out as a surprising visual encounter. The project, as a prototype, also starts to address other questions that arise in considering the conflicted perception of urban bat habitats, such as the possible presence of guano. Bat Cloud proposes a cyclical system, in which a 'planter' filled with soil and vegetation is situated at the lower portion of each pod, as a potential collector of guano, that could serve to fertilise any plants that might begin to grow in the suspended baskets.

The installation of Bat Cloud has provoked a number of reactions from the local community in Buffalo, as well as individuals engaged in ecological research and artistic production. We have received messages from a range of people, including

Above: Ants of the Prairie, Bat Cloud, 2012. As seen in February 2013, Buffalo, NY.

Below: Ants of the Prairie, Bat Cloud, 2012. View from walking trail in Tifft Nature Preserve, Buffalo, NY.

104   Working at the Intersection: Architecture After the Anthropocene

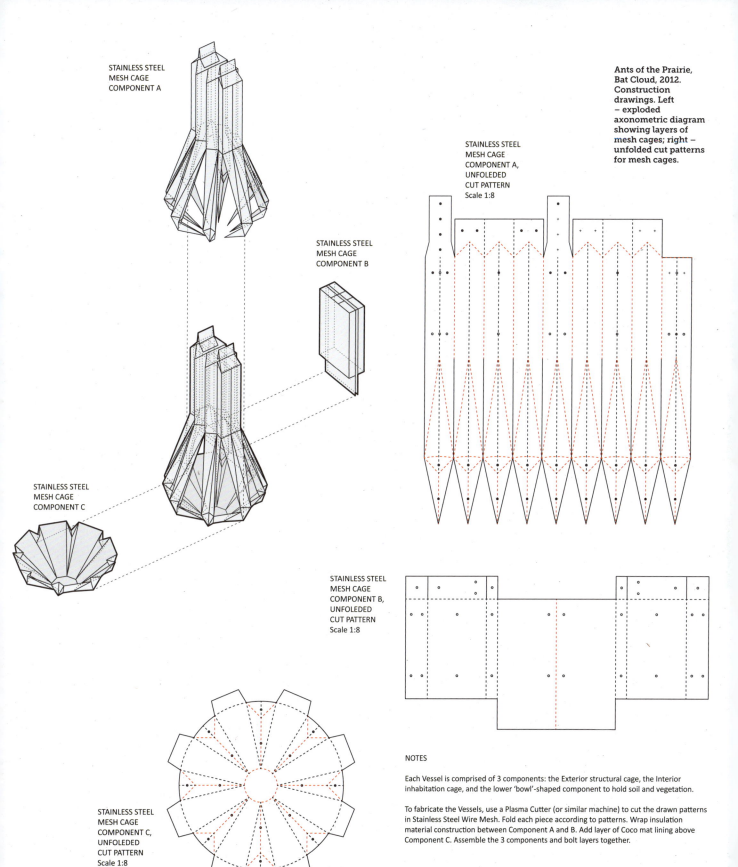

Ants of the Prairie, Bat Cloud, 2012. Construction drawings. Left – exploded axonometric diagram showing layers of mesh cages; right – unfolded cut patterns for mesh cages.

NOTES

Each Vessel is comprised of 3 components: the Exterior structural cage, the Interior inhabitation cage, and the lower 'bowl'-shaped component to hold soil and vegetation.

To fabricate the Vessels, use a Plasma Cutter (or similar machine) to cut the drawn patterns in Stainless Steel Wire Mesh. Fold each piece according to patterns. Wrap insulation material construction between Component A and B. Add layer of Coco mat lining above Component C. Assemble the 3 components and bolt layers together.

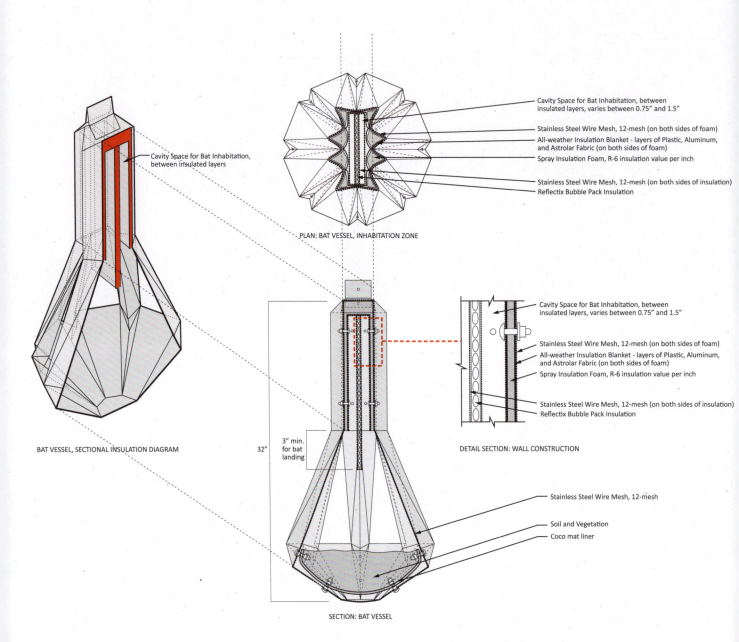

Above: Ants of the Prairie, Bat Cloud, 2012. Construction drawings.

Opposite: Ants of the Prairie, Bat Cloud, 2012. Bat Cloud with installation assistants Joey Swerdlin and Shawn Lewis in the foreground.

local residents enquiring about whether the pods are 'for sale', high school students interested in bat habitats, and even Scouts requesting advice in the design of bat houses for their projects. In 2014, a second iteration of Bat Cloud was fabricated and installed in the Netherlands as part of the International Architecture Biennale Rotterdam, and was later installed in Rotterdam's Pompenburg Park, suspended under a pedestrian bridge in the park's Peace Garden site. Most recently, in 2019, a representative from Tifft Nature Preserve informed us that a biology professor from a regional university was conducting a bat survey around the installation and reported bats flying in and out of the project. Our aim is to continue conversations with Tifft to learn from the extended research around Bat Cloud.

Credits
Ants of the Prairie
Project Director: Joyce Hwang
Project Design and Fabrication Manager (Buffalo): Sze Wan Li-Bain
Project Design and Fabrication Manager (Rotterdam): Joseph Swerdlin
Design and Fabrication Assistants: Mikaila Waters, Robert Yoos, Molly Hogle, Duane Warren, Shawn Lewis, Ian Liu, Andrews Santandreu
Additional Installation Assistants: Matthieu Bain, Joshua Gardner, Sergio López-Piñeiro, Nellie Niespodzinski, Mark Nowaczyk, Alex Poklinkowski, Duane Warren
Consultants
Structural Engineer: Mark Bajorek
Biologist: Katharina Dittmar
Event/Site Coordination and Support
UB Humanities Institute Fluid Culture organisers: Colleen Culleton, Justin Read
Tifft Nature Preserve/Buffalo Musuem of Science coordinators: Lauren Makeyenko, David Spiering
Support by: UB School of Architecture and Planning (Buffalo), Awesome Without Borders/Harnisch Foundation, IABR, ZUS (Rotterdam)

CASE STUDY: Bat Cloud

Hood Design Studio, Nvidia Headquarters, Santa Clara, CA, 2016 – ongoing. Site plan rendering provides an overview of the campus, which is about 4 acres.

CASE STUDY:
In Between Landscape

Walter Hood
Nvidia Headquarters, Santa Clara, CA, USA

Opposite: Hood Design Studio, Nvidia Headquarters, Santa Clara, CA, 2016 – ongoing. Aerial view of photovoltaic canopy.

Below: Hood Design Studio, Nvidia Headquarters, Santa Clara, CA, 2016 – ongoing. A large treehouse under the PV canopy.

Architecture's ability to adapt to environmental conditions can be the hallmark of invention. The twentieth century produced infrastructures that separated communities from the environments in which they lived. The consequences have been devastating, particularly to communities with few choices. Whether conditioned air, mechanical heating systems or prefabricated building systems, standardised buildings are advocated, no matter what the environmental context may be. In the same environments where historically inert materials such as stone or brick were used because of local sourcing and extreme weather conditions, we now see standardised metal and wood frame buildings springing up. In environments where local conditions prevail, freeze-thaw, heat, humidity, hydrology and so on once prompted designers to utilise passive solutions for environmental systems. Since their advent, the air-conditioner and slab-on-grade construction practices have spurned approaches to passive solutions and have instead bolstered a reliance on energy for cooling. More than 75% of US households use air-conditioners, and the US leads the world in air-conditioning use. When energy grids collapse, and when extreme weather events occur, architecture is left as the detritus of our achievements and failures.

CASE STUDY: In Between Landscape

During the Anthropocene architecture's eminence has been lost. The thickness of a wall has importance to what stays in and what stays out, and the importance of a roof, whether tilted, flat or cantilevered, or the importance of the ground, have all been abandoned for the sake of homogeneity and standardisation. Can we recover this eminence in the twenty-first century? Can we look more to place and the specificity of environment?

Nvidia's new campus landscape in Santa Clara, CA blurs the line between building and landscape, exploring the intersection between office space inside and outside. In an environment that hosts at least 261 days a year of sunshine (the average in the US is 205) and is one of the more comfortable environments in California, the design team was charged to take advantage of the outdoor context – not for leisure, as you see in most Silicon Valley tech campuses, but for work. Compressed between two office buildings that total nearly 160,000 square metres of office space and up to 6,000 employees per day, pre-Covid pandemic, a four-acre landscape mediates between the two. The buildings, built in phases, allowed the landscape to learn from the patterns and practices of employees after moving into the first phase. The landscape is a hybrid expression of both building and site. Inspired by the shade and growing structures of California's agrarian cultural landscape, a giant trellis organises the site, shading and powering the site and building through photovoltaics. A linear set of landforms divide the site, reinforcing its phasing and engaging the two different building thresholds that extend the ground landscape into each building. An above-ground floating walkway engages the pre-existing building that emerged from phase one, linking it to the phase two structure. Two treehouses anchor the walkway to the landscape, modifying California's flora, geology and microclimate.

Amphitheatre-inspired spaces for larger meetings and gatherings are integrated with the landscape's hydrological system, merging flora and fauna with human interaction. The landscape is designed spatially so that employees can find spaces that suit their work needs, whether for small or larger teams. Two and a half acres are used for these varied spaces. Smaller trellises at ground level are integrated with seating decks and stone boulders for more informal workspaces, and larger areas are adjacent to the building's threshold where food and beverage spaces converge. Up above, the treehouses orbit the site's two sides, projecting each building out into the landscape. The smaller treehouse connects the phase one building to the landscape, with a stepped amphitheatre and council ring at the ground level. Here, workers are embedded in the landscape, which offers a multiplicity of spatial arrangements. The large treehouse connects the phase two building and has a large deck that offers a view over to the cafeteria area and the Santa Clara hills. The landscape's eminence is characterised by the scale of walls, planting, treehouses and trellis. You know that they are doing work.

Top to bottom: Hood Design Studio, Nvidia Headquarters, Santa Clara, CA, 2016 – ongoing.

The overlook uses oversized platforms that run adjacent to the treehouse. Here they replace stairways as vertical connectors and serve as places to stage impromptu meetings and interactions.

Walkway connecting treehouses and main building. This campus investigates the relationship between inside/outside, workplace/collaboration and building/landscape.

Seating and lounge area inside the treehouse.

The seating and lounge area within the treehouse was designed to encourage both work collaboration and leisure.

Left: Hood Design Studio, Nvidia Headquarters, Santa Clara, CA, 2016 – ongoing. Recalling the agricultural roots of Santa Clara, the architects envision the trellis as more than a fundamental structure for agriculture. It yields an emotional response, which occurs while sitting under a canopy of vines, providing dappled shade, a myriad of green tones and a cool breeze.

Below: Hood Design Studio, Nvidia Headquarters, Santa Clara, CA, 2016 – ongoing. Here the landscape is seen as both apparatus and field as it entangles architecture, dissipates towards the sky and bleeds out to the horizon.

CASE STUDY: In Between Landscape

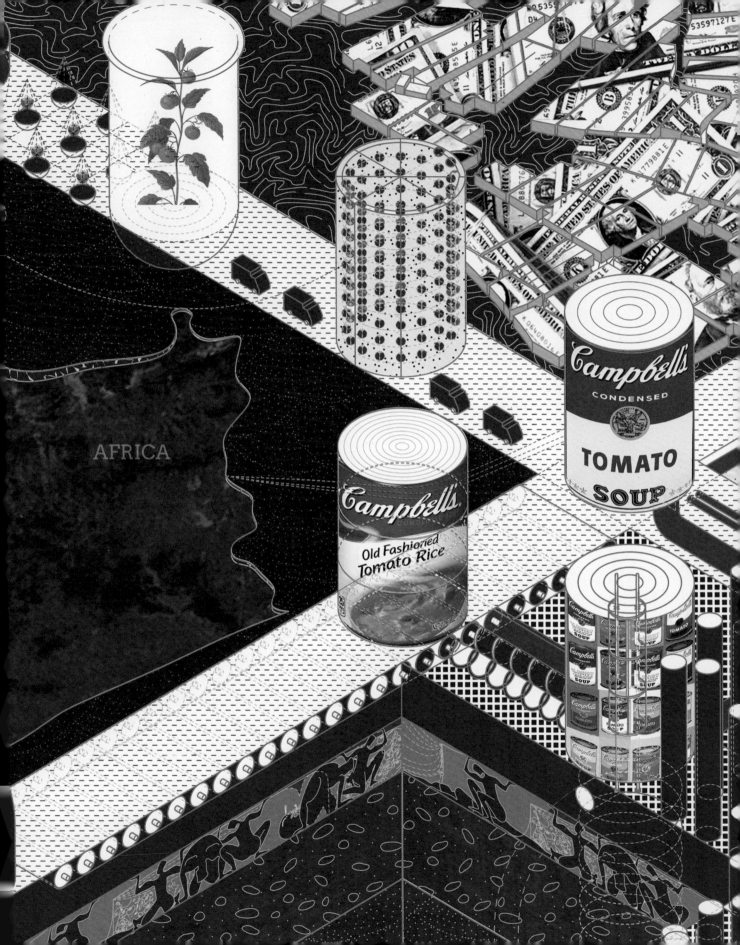

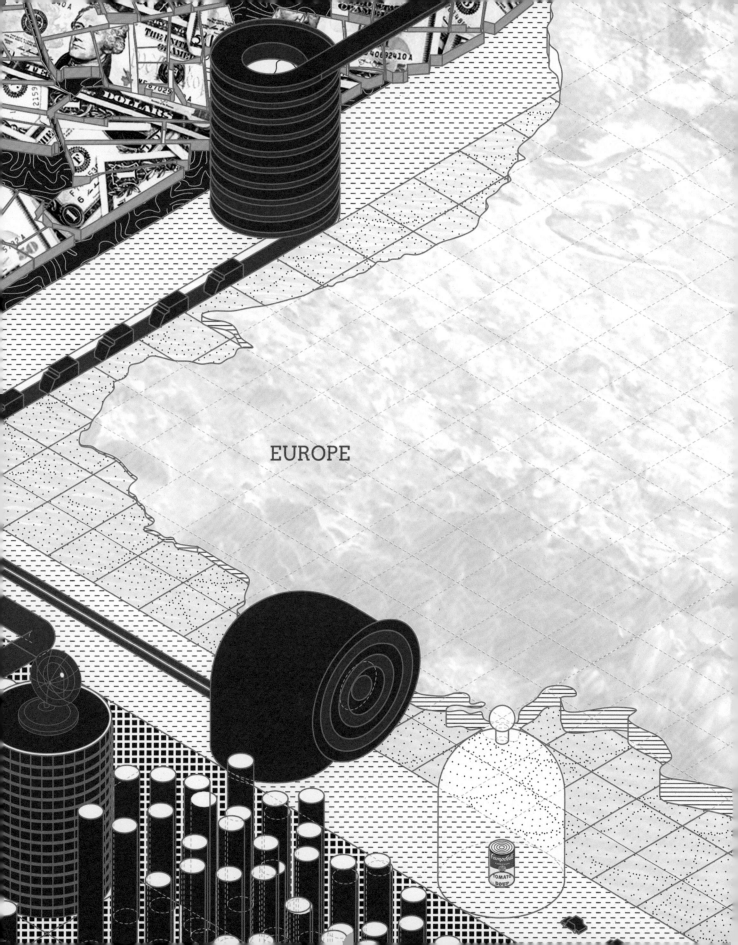

Previous spread:
Invisible Landscapes

Left: Indexical Ice

116

Final Word

Playful Seriousness Versus Serious Playfulness or, Socialism Versus Facism

Timothy Morton

Architecture is made of social relations. Social relations are made out of human and non-human beings. A radical change in how humans relate with one another and with non-human beings will thus change architecture. A more just co-existence between and among humans and non-humans is what I call an ecologically attuned society.

The current biosphere crisis requires a far more ecologically attuned society. Thank you for reading, you may email me at tbm2@rice.edu.

All right, all right – you've convinced me that you want a higher-resolution pass over this stuff. So.

What we are facing, in these 2020s in particular, is a very stark choice between the past and the future. Carry on doing what we're doing, and face biosphere collapse. Do something different, and have a chance to create something better for all lifeforms.

What we're doing includes the thing called neoliberal capitalism. Capitalism itself isn't just what has been the case. Capitalism is an algorithm. It's based on the past. An algorithm is a recipe. Take an egg, put it in boiling water, wait five minutes, remove the egg – that's a way to boil an egg at my altitude here in Houston, Texas. It's based on past attempts to boil eggs. A price is a reflection of the past states of a commodity. We are worried about automation because capitalism is already a form of automation. We are concerned about AI because we are already living inside an AI. We have been living inside this AI since the invention of the steam engine enabled capitalism to become automated. What is being automated? In a word, slavery. There is always one commodity that has to price itself lower than it should: human labour. Then capitalism requires a whole lot of other labour that doesn't even have a wage: the stuff that all other lifeforms do. Wheat doesn't charge a fee. You don't tip a forest for letting you breathe.

If Marx had had access to the phrase 'adaptive AI' and the phrase 'machine learn' he would've been able to put the first volume of *Capital* on the back of a matchbox: *capitalism is an adaptive AI that machine learns how to extract life from the biosphere without stopping*. It's that last part that is most concerning. Capitalism has to make more of itself in order to exist. It doesn't have a thermostat. It's those Mickey Mouse Sorcerer's Apprentice brooms from the film *Fantasia*. They just keep multiplying. It's on us to switch capitalism off. If we want to.

The *machine learn* part of the basic idea is disturbing too. It means *efficiency*. At a certain scale, efficiency might be the equivalent of evil. Efficiency is definitely based on the past: it means doing the same thing, better. Ecologically just worlds are not based on efficiency. They are not based on the past. They are based on the future, which is to say that they are based on *creativity*. Creativity implies failure, false starts, trial and error. At planet scale, every decision will have an obvious flaw. You can't get it 100% right: there is no one solution to rule them all. I think this is what socialism might actually feel like.

To us, gaslit by hundreds of years of efficiency, a different world might look really bad, just like how STEM makes arts and humanities look bad. But it is exactly this world that we require, like, now. How do you get there from here?

Luckily, time is not a Wikipedia timeline. The past is not a dot to the left on that line, and the future is not a dot to the right. Or a region. Timelines and grids and other tools are there to enable us to do stuff. The same goes for the concept we call *the present*. You can scale it to any size you want. If you're an electron, your present is nanoseconds. If you're the East India Company, your present is as long as it takes you to get around the Cape of Good Hope with all those new ships and credit instruments and perspective geometry to enable you to kick off the colonial period also known as *primitive accumulation*: the amassing of a giant pile of wealth that you can then use to automate the slavery later on.

The present is overrated, as anyone who actually meditates will tell you. The power of now is actually that it doesn't really have any power at all: it's just a feeling of relative motion, like walking up the down escalator. Relative motion between what? Between the past and the future, sliding over each other, overlapping, not touching. The esoteric meditation manuals tell you to drop the so-called present moment as well as the past and the future.

How things appear is the past. *What things are* is the future. The deliberate mistake of all world religions is to locate what things really are in the past. The deliberate tactic of fascism is to find meaning in the past. But meaning – what this sentence is really saying, is (in) the future, not the predictable one that you just build out from the past, but the genuinely future future, a radically unpredictable one in which you can never really know in advance how this sentence will elephant banana exceptionalism toilet parenthesis …

And as you can see from these sentences, the future is not over the edge of them, off in the distance, a vanishing point or dot, a promised land. It overlaps the appearance of things, the squiggles you're reading. The meaning is not 'in' the squiggles, but it overlaps them.

This is a sentence about the future. All sentences are from the future as well as from the past.

So, the future is everywhere. It's just invisible, that's all. Or less visible. It's the way this sentence shimmers with meaning, like a mirage. It doesn't seem so solid. It is most powerfully described in African philosophy as the Kalunga, the gate between the worlds. Ever so handily we have all seen this Kalunga. It has the form of the inside of a spiral shell and it's made of blue liquid – it's the *Star Wars* hyperspace tunnel. I'll see your fascist MAGA wear and I'll raise you a hyperspace tunnel. It's too late really, even for those MAGA people. Billions of people have seen the Kalunga. I don't know whether George Lucas was deliberately appropriating this concept, but it's stunning that his hyperspace is exactly like the gate between the worlds. And it's everywhere – that's the lesson of Afrofuturism. Hyperspace is everywhere. You just have to know how to find it, how to peel open the past with something like what Philip Pullman calls *the subtle knife*, peel it open and slip into it.

I'm making it sound too sci-fi, really. What if was only too easy to slip in? What if people like me frequently thought that we got paid to say how hard it was, or even impossible? And words like 'in' are so compromised, part of how the measurement of time has covered over time, mostly because so-called western so-called civilisation has been so busy, busy, busy with its various projects, such as generating patriarchy, class division, slavery and speciesism.

The future is everywhere, and it's infinite, in the true sense – you can't count it in advance. Same with the past. There's an infinity of broken bits called the past lying around. I look at my face in the mirror. It's a map of everything that ever happened to my face: that terrible acne I had when I was nineteen, that makeup I just put on. My face is the past. But what is this face? Who is this Tim Morton? That's the future. My face is the future.

Everywhere you look, you find the past. But if you keep on looking you might discern how things are always evaporating, there's an inaccessible pathway just out of sight, a secret door hiding in plain sight, the possibility that things can be different, shimmering everywhere like an illusion. You might not believe it because of that. People like me often think they get paid to make sure you don't believe in this Kalunga. That the past is so paralysingly 'there' that really, how dare you imagine an exit? *You have no idea just how paralysed you are. Therefore I am more intelligent than you.* That's most of what passes these days for theory class, in two sentences.

Words are funny. Words are from the past. Words are therefore compromised. But you have to use them. The word *non-human* is a funny, compromised word. *Symbiosis* and *evolution* mean that these so-called non-humans *are me* as much as my human DNA, and so on.

On the other hand I am, so they tell me, a philosopher. Philosophy means the love of wisdom. Many young men seem to think it means having big ideas and then comparing the size of their big ideas with other young men's big ideas. *Philos* means love and *sophy* means wisdom. There's nothing about big ideas in there. That word is more like two emotions, fused together. If you had a choice between calling wisdom an idea or set of ideas on the one hand, and a feeling or feel on the other, you would have to say it's the latter. It's the last syllable of that word that wags the dog: '-dom' like the '-ence' in intelligence, which makes it quite different from *intellect*. A feeling, or feel, or affect as some prefer to say. And as for love …

And feelings are (from) the future. That's why you think of going to therapy. You're having a feeling that you don't quite know how to put into words. The ideas are all (from) the past. They're just the receipts that come out of the cash register at the end of the transaction. The hyperobject feeling is much more important than the word *hyperobject*, and now we know exactly what that is – it's called coronavirus. Philosophy doesn't mean having (big) ideas. It means letting yourself not have them. Relax, don't have one. You're holding open the door called the future. The possibility that things can be different. You're doing something much more pleasant than having ideas. You're making nice allergy medicine so people don't have an allergic reaction to the ambiguous, shimmery future-ness. You're interfering with the whole idea that things can be bought and sold for a specific price. You're interfering with the past, and with economic and social systems based on the past.

A socialist future would feel more creative. It would therefore feel more hesitant, more awkward perhaps, beset with false starts and failures, just like when you do a drawing.

So, we have this choice between serious playfulness – which is how Google operates – and playful seriousness – which is how creativity operates.

Serious playfulness is what I saw at the Capitol on 6 January 2021, the event the *Times of India* called the *Coup Klux Klan*.[1] Fascist clowns, serious clowns, deadly serious. That moment when the clowns force you into audience participation. Dressing up in the past was always part of the violence. The Tea Party was always about partying like it was 1775, a time when actual slavery was totally legal in America.

Black Lives Matter. Wouldn't that be great? The phrase is from the future. The *life* in that phrase is very significant. It's not life versus non-life. It's not an idea. It's a feeling, that feeling we call *alive* rather than the overkill, death-drive state called *survival*. The default state of art is dance, because it's all really about how you hold and move your body, from paintings in white cubes to social protest as art. And the default state of dance is called being alive. Often this is quite habitual – you wake up, grab a coffee and head for the subway station. It's a boring dance, perhaps, but it's still dancing. And the default state of alive is called being asleep. Your body is just vibrating all by itself, your brain is dreaming … which is its way of doing that shimmer that your heart is also doing.

The Greek for this kind of life isn't *bios*, the concept of life versus non-life. It isn't *zoe*, the concept of bare life, the kind you can execute at will if you've organised the rules that way. The Greek for this kind of life is *thumos*. *Thumos* is the life you mean when you touch your chest as you're having an emotion. It's moving, pulsing, palpitating, vibrating. It's in the last syllable of the word *rhythm*. This is the life that non-violent direct action resorts to, the body as 'dead weight', just living, in the street. It's a dance, dance at its ground state, just being alive, being inert with the fluids pulsing. The shimmering doorway of the future.

---

1 Chidanand Rajghatta, 'Coup Klux Klan: Don triggers mob and rob bid', *Times of India*, 8 January 2021, https://timesofindia.indiatimes.com/world/us/coup-klux-klan-don-triggers-mob-rob-bid/articleshow/80161869.cms.

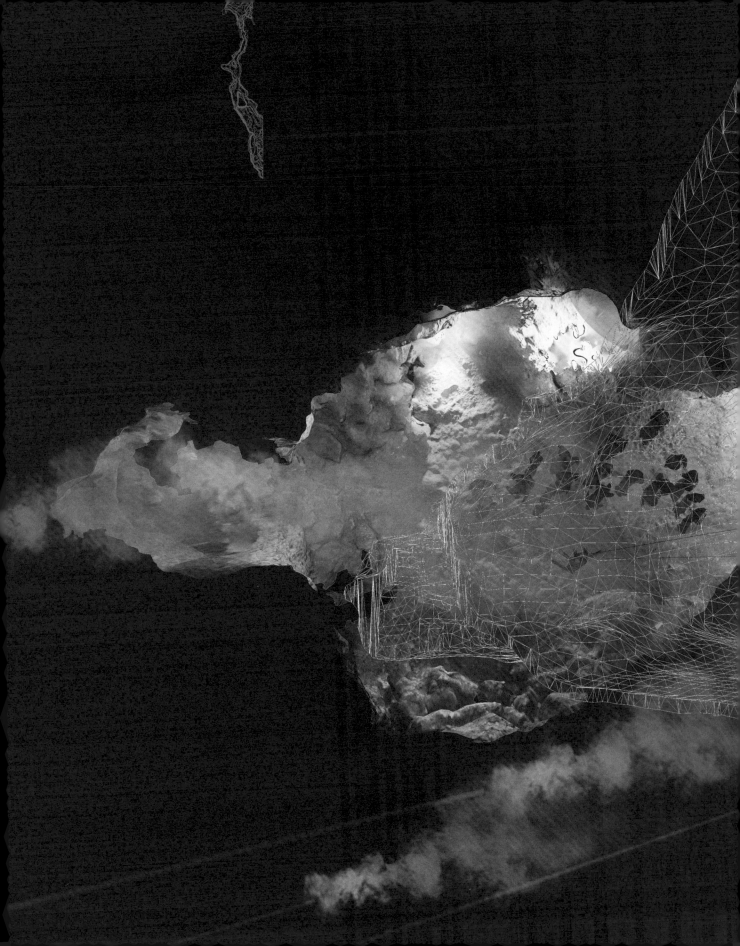

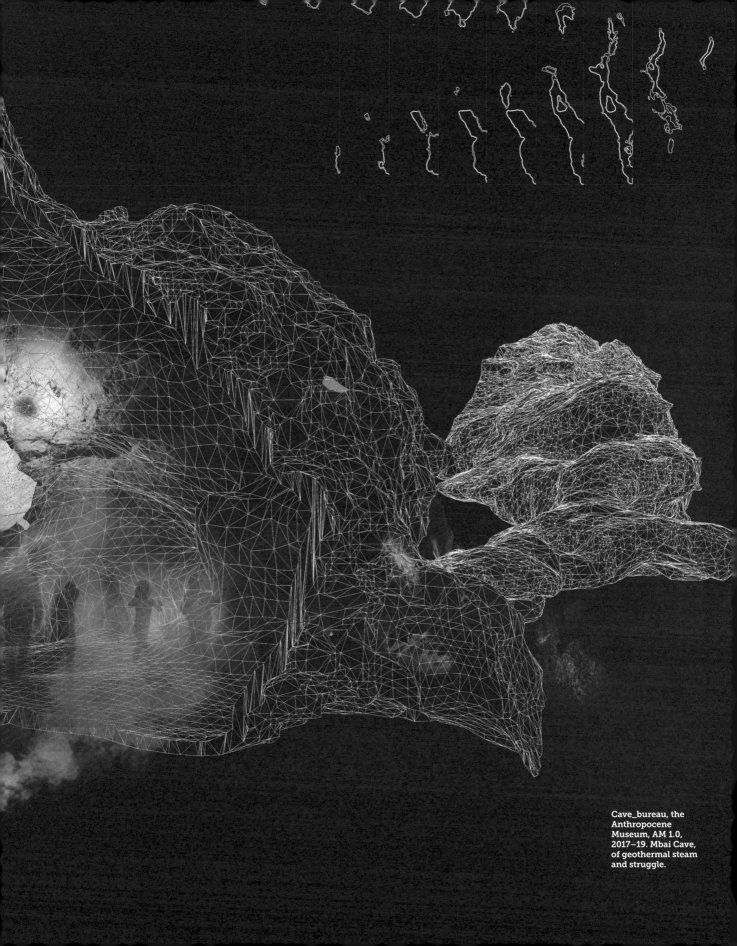

Cave_bureau, the Anthropocene Museum, AM 1.0, 2017–19. Mbai Cave, of geothermal steam and struggle.

Contributors

Marcos Cruz is an architect and Professor of Innovative Environments at the Bartlett, UCL. His main research focuses on bio-integrated design in buildings. He runs Bio-ID with Dr Brenda Parker, a multidisciplinary research platform and Master's programme that investigates design driven by advances in biotechnology, computation, materials and fabrication. He was co-editor of Syn.de.Bio and founder of the BiotA Lab (2014–18).

Casper Laing Ebbensgaard is a cultural geographer and Leverhulme Early Career Fellow at Queen Mary University of London and lecturer in geography at University of East Anglia. His research explores the aesthetic and affective politics of architecture, urban design and urban planning practice. He is currently working on the project Luminous Verticality: The changing geographies of East London at night.

Antón García-Abril and **Débora Mesa** are architects and founders of Ensamble Studio, based in Madrid, Spain. Their work addresses issues as diverse as the construction of the landscape to the prefabrication of a house. Antón and Débora are committed to sharing ideas and cultivating synergies between professional and academic worlds through teaching, lecturing and researching: she is Ventulett Chair in Architectural Design at Georgia Tech and he is a professor at MIT, where they co-founded the POPlab (Prototypes of Prefabrication Laboratory) in 2012.

Ariane Lourie Harrison is an architect and Visiting Associate Professor of Graduate Architecture and Urban Design at Pratt Institute in New York. A principal and co-founder of Harrison Atelier, her projects and writing explore the concepts and realities of making architecture for multiple species, from her anthology *Architectural Theories of the Environment: Posthuman Territory* (Routledge, 2013) to 'Feral Architecture', in *Aesthetics Equals Politics* (MIT Press, 2019).

Kerry Holden is a lecturer in human geography at Queen Mary University of London. Her research interests are in exploring knowledge cultures and practices transnationally. She focuses on examining the managerial, administrative and professional dimensions of science and technology, analysing the significance of political and moral economies that support how science travels and becomes politically viable.

Walter Hood is an architect and creative director and founder of Hood Design Studio in Oakland, California. He is also a Professor at the University of California, Berkeley, and lectures on professional and theoretical projects nationally and internationally. He is a recipient of the Academy of Arts and Letters Architecture Award (2017), the Knight Public Spaces Fellowship (2019), the MacArthur Fellowship (2019), the Dorothy and Lillian Gish Prize (2019) and the Architectural League President's Medal (2021).

Joyce Hwang is Associate Professor of Architecture at the University at Buffalo SUNY and the director of Ants of the Prairie. She is a recipient of the Architectural League Emerging Voices Award (2014), the New York Foundation for the Arts Fellowship (2013) and the MacDowell Fellowship (2011, 2016). Hwang received an MArch degree from Princeton University and a BArch degree from Cornell University.

Kabage Karanja and **Stella Mutegi** are founders and directors of Cave_bureau, a collective of architects and researchers based in Nairobi, Kenya that maps explorations of nature's architecture and urbanism. Their studies examine the African city's anthropological and geological context as a way of resolving the problems of contemporary rural and urban life.

V. Mitch McEwen is an architect, urban planner and cultural activist. Assistant Professor of Architecture at Princeton University, she is co-founder of Atelier Office, an architecture collaborative of studios in Detroit, Los Angeles and Brooklyn. McEwen's design work has been awarded grants from the Graham Foundation, Knight Foundation and New York State Council on the Arts.

Timothy Morton is a professor and Rita Shea Guffey Chair in English at Rice University, Houston, Texas, working at the intersection between object-oriented thinking and ecological studies. Morton is the author of a number of publications including *Being Ecological* (Penguin,

2018), *Humankind: Solidarity with Nonhuman People* (Verso, 2017), *Dark Ecology: For a Logic of Future Coexistence* (Columbia University Press, 2016) and *Hyperobjects: Philosophy and Ecology after the End of the World* (University of Minnesota Press, 2013).

Brenda Parker is a lecturer in biochemical engineering at University College London. Her current research seeks to address the need for sustainable and scalable platforms for industrial biotechnology and biorefining. She founded the Living Designs forum to bring together scientists, engineers, architects and designers, and collaborates with the Bartlett School of Architecture and the Slade School of Art at UCL, on projects relating to microalgae.

Carolyn Steel is a leading thinker on food and cities. A London-based architect and academic, she is the author of *Hungry City: How Food Shapes Our Lives* (Chatto & Windus, 2008) and *Sitopia: How Food Can Save the World* (Chatto & Windus, 2020). Her 2009 TED talk has received more than one million views.

McKenzie Wark is a writer and academic best known for her work in critical theory and new media. Professor of Culture and Media and programme director of gender studies at the New School, New York, she is author of a number of publications including *A Hacker Manifesto* (Harvard University Press, 2004), *Gamer Theory* (Harvard University Press, 2007) and more recently *Capital is Dead* (Verso Books, 2019) and *Reverse Cowgirl* (MIT Press, 2020).

Kathryn Yusoff is Professor of Inhuman Geography at Queen Mary University of London. Her work is centred on dynamic Earth events such as abrupt climate change, biodiversity loss and extinction. She is interested in how these 'Earth revolutions' impact social thought. Broadly, her work has focused on political aesthetics, social theory and abrupt environmental change.

Joanna Zylinska is a writer, lecturer, artist and curator, working in the areas of digital technologies and new media, ethics, photography and art. She is Professor of Media Philosophy + Critical Digital Practice at King's College London. The author of a number of books – including *The End of Man: A Feminist Counterapocalypse* (2018), *Nonhuman Photography* (2017) and *Minimal Ethics for the Anthropocene* (2014) – her art practice involves working with different forms of image-based media.

Recommended Reading

Books

Carol J Adams, *The Sexual Politics of Meat: A Feminist-Vegetarian Critical Theory*, London, Bloomsbury Academic, 2015.

Stacy Alaimo, *Bodily Natures: Science, Environment, and the Material Self*, Bloomington, IN, Indiana University Press, 2010.

Jane Bennett, *Vibrant Matter: A Political Ecology of Things*, Durham and London, Duke University Press, 2010.

Judith Butler, *Senses of the Subject*, New York, Fordham University Press, 2015.

Octavia E Butler, *The Parable of the Sower*, New York, Grand Central Publishing, 2019.

Marisol de la Cadena and Mario Blaser, eds, *A World of Many Worlds*, Durham and London, Duke University Press, 2018.

Kimberlé Crenshaw, *On Intersectionality: Essential Writings*, New York, The New Press, 2017.

Arturo Escobar, *Designs for the Pluriverse: Radical Interdependence, Autonomy and the Making of Worlds*, Durham, NC, Duke University Press, 2018.

David Graeber: *The Dawn of Everything*. Allen Lane London 2021.

Richard Grusin, ed., *After Extinction*, Minneapolis, University of Minnesota Press, 2018.

Richard Grusin, ed., *Anthropocene Feminism*, Minneapolis and London, University of Minnesota Press, 2017.

Donna Haraway, *Staying with the Trouble: Making Kin in the Chthulucene*, Durham and London, Duke University Press, 2016.

John Hartigan Jr., *Aesop's Anthropology: A Multispecies Approach*, Minneapolis, University of Minnesota Press, 2014.

Tim Ingold, *Lines: A Brief History*, Abingdon, Routledge, 2016.

Naomi Klein, *This Changes Everything: Capitalism vs. the Climate*, London, Penguin Books, 2015.

Bruno Latour, *Down to Earth: Politics in the New Climatic Regime*, Cambridge, Polity Press, 2019.

Bruno Latour, *Facing Gaia: Eight Lectures on the New Climatic Regime*, Cambridge, Polity Press, 2017.

Sherilyn MacGregor, ed., *Routledge Handbook of Gender and Environment*, Abingdon, Routledge, 2017.

Brian Massumi, *What Animals Teach us about Politics*, Durham and London, Duke University Press, 2014.

Katherine McKittrick, ed., *Sylvia Wynter: On Being Human as Praxis*, Durham and London, Duke University Press, 2015.

Timothy Morton, *Dark Ecology: For a Logic of Future Coexistence*, New York, Columbia University Press, 2018.

Heike Munder and Suad Garayeva-Maleki, *Potential Worlds: Planetary Memories and Eco-Fictions*, Zurich, Scheidegger & Spiess, 2020.

Nicolas Nova, ed., *A Bestiary of the Anthropocene*, Eindhoven, Onomatopee, 2021.

Richard Powers, *Bewilderment*, Heinemann, 2021.

Nicole Seymour, *Strange Natures - Futurity, Empathy, and the Queer Ecological Imagination*, Urbana, Chicago and Springfield, University of Illinois Press, 2013.

Kim Stanley Robinson, *The Ministry of the Future*, London, Orbit, 2020.

Isabelle Stengers, *In Catastrophic Times: Resisting the Coming Barbarism*, Ann Arbor, MI, Open Humanities Press, University of Michigan Library, 2015.

Anna Lowenhaupt Tsing, Nils Bubandt, Elaine Gan and Heather Anne Swanson, *Arts of Living on a Damaged Planet: Ghosts and Monsters of the Anthropocene*, Minneapolis, University of Minnesota Press, 2017.

Etienne Turpin, ed., *Architecture in the Anthropocene: Encounters Among Design, Deep Time, Science and Philosophy*, Ann Arbor, MI, Open Humanities Press, University of Michigan Library, 2013.

Liam Young, ed., *Machine Landscapes: Architectures of the Post-Anthropocene (Architectural Design)*, Hoboken, NY, Wiley, 2019.

Kathryn Yusoff, *A Billion Black Anthropocenes or None*, Minneapolis, University of Minnesota Press, 2018.

Joanna Zylinska, *The End of Man: A Feminist Counter-Apocalypse*, Minneapolis, University of Minnesota Press, 2018.

Websites

The Institute of Queer Ecology: queerecology.org

The Expanded Environment: animalarchitecture.org

Feral Partnerships: feralpartnerships.com

Future Architecture: futurearchitectureplatform.org

Biodesigned: biodesigned.org

Climavore: climavore.org

Submission on Quarternary Stratigraphy: quaternary.stratigraphy.org/working-groups/anthropocene/

Territorial Agency: territorialagency.com

Forensic Architecture: forensic-architecture.org

Dark Matter University: darkmatteruniversity.org/

Blackspace: www.blackspace.org

Extinction Rebellion: rebellion.global

NASA's Global Icecap Viewer: climate.nasa.gov/interactives/global-ice-viewer/#/

Index

Page numbers in **bold** indicate figures.

Ahmed, Sara 43
air-conditioning 111
The Aircraft Carrier of Ice **14**
algae-laden hydrogel **54**, 57, **57**, 58
allotments 26, 69
Almere Oosterwold, Netherlands **70**, 71
#amazingdroneviews 35–36, **35**
analogous habitats 88–95, **88**, **89**, **90–91**, **92**, **93**, **94**
Anthropocene VIII, 73
Anthropocene Museum **72**, 73–79, **73**, **74**, **75**, **76**, **77**, **78**, **79**
Anthropocene Working Group (AWG) 73
antidiscrimination law 2, 3
Ants of the Prairie **102**, 103–107, **103**, **104**, **105**, **106**, **107**
Architectural Design 33
Aristotle 65, 66
asexual reproduction **27**, 28
assembly plants **XIV**, 3–7

bacteria **22–23**, 55
 see also cyanobacteria
Baldwin, James 45
Baloji, Sammy **44–45**, **46**, **50–51**
Bat Cloud, Buffalo, New York, USA **102**, 103–107, **103**, **104**, **105**, **106**, **107**
Batterie de Longues-sur-Mer, Normandy, France **13**
bees 92
 see also Pollinators Pavilion, Hudson, New York, USA
Bestiary of the Anthropocene, A (Nova) 24, **25**
biodesign 53
bio-integrated design 52–61
 biofabrication 53, 57, **57**, 60
 biogenic veneers 56, **56**
 biomineralisation **55**, 56
 biophotovoltaics 58, **58**
 bioprecipitation 56
 bioreceptivity **52**, **54**, 55, **55**
 bioremediation 58, **59**
 biosensors 58
 defining 53–54
 food-waste composites 58, **58**
 future buildings 60, **60**
 microbiomes 55

poikilohydric designs **52**, **54**, 55, **55**, 56
The Birds and the Bees project **90–91**, 93
Black feminism 1, 24
 see also intersectionality
boda bodas (motorcycle taxis) 48–49
Bohn, Katrin 71
Bohne, Matthew **90–91**
Braidotti, Rosi 38
Bridge, Gavin 42
Brooklyn Grange Rooftop Farm, New York City, USA **69**
Brooklyn Liberation for Black Trans Lives, New York, USA **19**
burial sites, historical mapping of 7–8, **7**

Ca'n Terra, Menorca **80**, 81–87, **81**, **82**, **83**, **84**, **85**, **86**, **87**
Capitalocene VIII
cat and anti-cat conundrum 22–23
Cave Canon at the Cascades exhibition 79
Cave_bureau **72**, 73–79, **73**, **74**, **75**, **76**, **77**, **78**, **79**
cemeteries, historical mapping of 7–8, **7**
Chevrolet **XIV**, 3, 6–7
Chicago Union Stockyards, USA **62–63**
chimera 24
Chthulucene VIII, 73–74, 79
civil rights law 2, 3
colonialism 29, 73, 74–75
 see also planetary portals
Constant's New Babylon (Widgery) 12–13, 16
Cooper Hewitt, Smithsonian Design Museum, New York City, USA 79
Corvette 6–7
Covid-19 pandemic 65, 71
CPULs (Continuous Productive Urban Landscapes) 71
Crenshaw, Kimberlé 1, 2, 3, 8
critical race theory 2, 3
Crutzen, Paul J. 73
Cube Museum, Kerkrade, Netherlands 79
cyanobacteria **55**, 56

data server centres 47–48
Davis, G. H. **14**
De Boeck, Filip 45

Death Alley, Louisiana, USA 7–8, **7**, **9**
Death of a Discipline (Spivak) 35
DeGraffenreid v. General Motors 2, 3, 6
Desprez, Louis Jean **24**
double separation 3
drone images
 #amazingdroneviews 35–36, **35**
 Feminist with a Drone project 36–38, **36**, **37**
 'loser images' figuration 38–39, **38**, **39**
dysphoria 18

Easterling, Keller 47
Eaton, Severn **25**, **30**
embedded ecologies 55
energy, biophotovoltaics 58, **58**
engineered living material (ELM) **55**, 56
Ensamble Studio **80**, 81–87, **81**, **82**, **83**, **84**, **85**, **86**, **87**
environmental racism VIII, xi, 7–8, **7**, **9**
exoelectrogenic activity 58
extraction, architectures of see planetary portals

Falling House, The (Tayou) 49
Fanon, Franz 46
feminist theory 1, 24, 38
 see also intersectionality
Feminist with a Drone project 36–38, **36**, **37**
Fertile Crescent 63
Flanner, Ben 69
Flusser, Vilém 36
The Food Movement 71
food systems 62–71, **62–63**
 transformation in 69–71, **69**, **70**
 urban paradox **64**, 65–66
 utopian thought 66–69, **67**, **68**
food-waste composites 58, **58**
Forensic Architecture 1, 7–8, **7**, **9**
Foster, John Bellamy 16
fungi **20–21**, **22–23**, 26, **27**, **27**, 29
futurity **25**, **25**

Gabrys, Jennifer 46
garden cities 66–69
Garden Cities of To-Morrow (Howard) 66, **68**

126

Working at the Intersection: Architecture After the Anthropocene

gender dysphoria 18
General Motors **XIV**, 2, 3, 6–7
geodetic markers **46**
George, Henry 66
Ghosh, Amitav 75
Gibson, James 35–36
Gill-Peterson, Jules 16
Google 47
Great Derangement, Climate Change and the Unthinkable, The (Ghosh) 75
Greeks, ancient 65, 66
Guggenheim Museum, New York City, USA **28**, 79

'Habitat 1: Regenerative Interactive Zone of Nurture' **28**
Hall, Gary 39
Haraway, Donna 21, 38, 73–74, 75
Harrison Atelier 88–95, **88**, **89**, **90–91**, **92**, **93**, **94**, **95**
high-rise buildings 42, **44–45**, 45–46
homosexual activity 28
Hood Design Studio **108–109**, 109–113, **110**, **111**, **112**, **113**
hormones 15–16
House of the Earth *see* Ca'n Terra, Menorca
Howard, Ebenezer 66–69, **68**
Human Rights Watch 7
Hurricane Katrina 15–16, **15**
hybridity 24, **24**, **25**, 26
hyperobjectivity 29
hyper-waste-objects 29, **30**

Ingels, Bjarke VIII
International Architecture Biennale Rotterdam 107
intersectionality VII–VIII, 1–9
  assembly plants **XIV**, 3–7
  critical race theory 2, 3
  double separation 3
  environmental racism VIII, XI, 7–8, **7**, **9**
  modernity and 2–3
  plastics industry **4–5**, 7–8, **7**, **9**
iPhone 46–47

kainotecture 11–18
Khan, Albert 6–7
Kimberley Mine, South Africa **42**, **43**, **46**, **48**
Kinshasa, Democratic Republic of the Congo **44–45**, 45, 48–49

Knepp Castle Estate, UK 71
Kurokawa, Kisho 10

Lamb, Sybil 15–16
Latour, Bruno 2, 3
Letchworth, Hertfordshire, UK 66–69
LiDAR technology 46–47
Liebig, Justus von 16
litter collectivism **20–21**, **22–23**, 26–28, **26**
Lokko, Lesley 73, 78, 79
'loser images' figuration 38–39, **38**, **39**

McLean, Heather 38
Mars **12**
  The Wilding of Mars (artwork) **96–97**, 97–101, **98**, **99**, **100**, **101**
Marx, Karl 12, 16, 18
Massey, Doreen 49
matsutake mushrooms 26
Mbai Caves, Kenya **73**, **75**, 79
Menorca *see* Ca'n Terra, Menorca
metabolic rift 16, 18
metabolism 11–18
Microbiome-Inspired Green Infrastructure (MIGI) 55
microplastics **4–5**, 8
Milan Food Pact 71
mines 17, **42**, **43**, 46–47, **46**, **48**, **50–51**
modernity 2–3
More, Thomas 66, **67**
mosses 26, 27, 28, 29
  bio-integrated design **52**, **54**, 55, **55**, 58
Mount Suswa, Kenya **77**, 79
Museum of Art, Architecture and Technology (MAAT), Lisbon 79
MVRDV **70**, 71
mycelia **20–21**, **22–23**, 27
mycorrhiza 26

Nairobi, Kenya 45
Nakagin Capsule Tower, Tokyo, Japan **10**
Nature 42
New Orleans, Louisiana, USA **15**
non-binary ecology 21–31
  hybridity 24, **24**, **25**, 26
  hyperobjectivity 29
  litter collectivism **20–21**, **22–23**, 26–28, **26**
  object-waste 29, **30**
  post futurities 25, **25**

precarity 26
  sexual systems **27**, 28
Nova, Nicolas 24, **25**
Nvidia Headquarters, Santa Clara, California, USA **108–109**, 109–113, **110**, **111**, **112**, **113**
Nye, David E 47

ocean pollution **4–5**, 8, 29
oikonomia 65–66, 69
Oreskes, Naomi 73

Parker, Barry 69
pedreras (quarries) *see* Ca'n Terra, Menorca
perception, visual 35–36
Petrini, Carlo 71
Petrochemical Corridor, Louisiana, USA 7–8, **7**, **9**
photosynthetic organisms *see* bio-integrated design
PigeonBlog **25**
Pirate Philosophy (Hall) 39
'Planetarity' (Spivak) 35
planetary images **32**, 33–39, **33**
  #amazingdroneviews 35–36, **35**
  Feminist with a Drone project 36–38, **36**, **37**
  'loser images' figuration 38–39, **38**, **39**
  Planetary Exhalation project **34**, 38
planetary portals 40–51
  data server centres 47–48
  high-rise buildings 42, **44–45**, 45–46
  mines **42**, **43**, 46–47, **46**, **48**, **50–51**
  portal as disruptive method 43
  resistance and survivalism 48–49
plants
  The Wilding of Mars (artwork) **96–97**, 97–101, **98**, **99**, **100**, **101**
  see also bio-integrated design; mosses
plastic pollution **4–5**, 8, 29
plastics industry **4–5**, 7–8, **7**, **9**
Plato 65, 66
poikilohydric designs **52**, **54**, 55, **55**, 56
Pollinators Pavilion, Hudson, New York, USA 88–95, **88**, **89**, **92**, **94**, **95**
pollution
  bioremediation 58, **59**

hyper-waste-objects 29, **30**
plastic **4–5**, 8, 29
Trash Island 29
Pompenburg Park, Rotterdam, Netherlands 107
portals *see* planetary portals
precarity 26
pre-knowledge 23
Progress and Poverty (George) 66

quarries *see* Ca'n Terra, Menorca
queer ecology *see* non-binary ecology

racial discrimination 2
   see also intersectionality
racial inequalities *see* planetary portals
racism, environmental VIII, XI, 7–8, **7**, **9**
Red Earth Project **40–41**
regenerative agriculture 69, 71, 93–94
RISE St. James 1, 7–8
Robinson, Kim Stanley 13
Rome, ancient **63**, 66
Rosenberg, Jordy 18
Rossi, Aldo 95

Salu, Michael **40–41**
Schrödinger's cat 22–23
sex discrimination 2
   see also intersectionality
sexology 16
sexual systems **27**, 28
Shimoni Slave Caves, Kenya **76**, **78–79**, 79
Simone, AbdouMaliq 46, 49
sitopia 62–71, **62–63**
   transformation in 69–71, **69**, **70**
   urban paradox **64**, 65–66
   utopian thought 66–69, **67**, **68**
skyscrapers 42, **44–45**, 45–46
Slow Food 71
Smith, Constance 45
solitary bees 92
   see also Pollinators Pavilion, Hudson, New York, USA
Species Wall, Clermont Historical Site, New York, USA 92–93, **93**
Spivak, Gayatri Chakravorty 35, 36
Stewart, Kathleen 49
Steyerl, Hito 33, 38–39

Subcommission on Quaternary Stratigraphy (SQS) 73
Syvitsky, Jaia 73

Tayou, Pascale Marthine 49
Technocene viii
Tifft Nature Preserve, Buffalo, New York, USA **102**, 103–107, **103**, **104**, **105**, **106**, **107**
The Tower, 7th Street, Limete, Kinshasa, Democratic Republic of the Congo **44–45**
trans people 13–16, 18, **19**
Transition Towns 71
Trash Island 29
Tresch, John 33
Tsing, Anna 73

Unwin, Raymond 69
urban farming 26, 69–71, **69**, **70**
Utopia (More) 66, **67**

Venice Biennale **77**, **78**, 79
Via Campesina 71
Viljoen, André 71
Virilio, Paul 13
visual perception 35–36

waste
   bioremediation 58, **59**
   food-waste composites 58, **58**
   hyper-waste-objects 29, **30**
   plastics **4–5**, 8, 29
   Trash Island 29
White Papers Black Marks (Lokko) 73, 78, 79
The Wilding of Mars (artwork) **96–97**, 97–101, **98**, **99**, **100**, **101**
Williams, Mark 73
World Around Summit 79

Young, Liam 33

Zalasiewicz, Jan 73

Image Credits

VI
NASA / GSFC
IX
Naveen Nkadalaveni, CC BY-SA 4.0, via Wikimedia Commons
X
Harris Brisbane Dick Fund, 1926, The Met Collection
XII
Athanasius Kircher, Wellcome Collection, Public Domain Mark
XIV
Photograph by Joseph Hampel, 1946. Missouri History Museum Photographs and Prints Collections. Joseph Hampel Album. NS 23696.
3
V Mitch McEwen
4, 5
FLPA / Alamy Stock Photo
7, 9
© FORENSIC ARCHITECTURE, 2021
10
RIBA Collections
12
Science History Images / Alamy Stock Photo
13
Jebulon, CC0, via Wikimedia Commons
14
© Illustrated London News Ltd/ Mary Evans
15
David Mark, via Pixabay
16, 19
McKenzie Wark
17
CSIRO, CC BY 3.0, via Wikimedia Commons
20, 21
Harriet Harriss and Severn Eaton
22, 23
Roy L. Moodie, Wellcome Collection, CC BY 4.0
24 top
Rijksmuseum, Purchased with the support of the F.G. Waller-Fonds
24 bottom
Nicolas Nova
25
Harriet Harriss and Naomi House
26
Joseph Reagle, CC BY-SA 4.0, via Wikimedia Commons
27
Janice Haney Carr, Robert Simmons, USCDCP, CC0
28
Institute of Queer Ecology
30
Severn Eaton
32, 33
NASA
34, 35, 36, 37, 38, 39
Joanna Zylinska
40, 41
Michael Salu
42
Chronicle / Alamy Stock Photo
43
The Diamond-field Keepsake for 1873, by MURRAY, Richard William, p.21. Original held and digitised by the British Library.
44, 45, 46 top, 50, 51
Sammy Baloji
46 bottom
Incwadi Yami; or, Twenty years' personal experience in South Africa, by MATTHEWS, Josiah Wright, p.167. Original held and digitised by the British Library.
48
Incwadi Yami; or, Twenty years' personal experience in South Africa, by MATTHEWS, Josiah Wright, p.127. Original held and digitised by the British Library.
52
Sarah Lever
54
Marcos Cruz
55 left
Alexandra Lăcătuşu
55 right
Prantar Tamuli
56
Nina Jotanovic
57, 58 right
Shneel Malik
58 left
Jingyuan Meng
59
Marcos Cruz and Shneel Malik
60
Ian Thomas Robinson
62, 63
Niday Picture Library / Alamy Stock Photo
64, 69
Carolyn Steel
67
Lebrecht Music & Arts / Alamy Stock Photo
68
Ebenezer Howard, Garden Cities of Tomorrow, Sonnenschein publishing, 1902. Reproduced by permission of the Town and Country Planning Association.
70
MVRDV Architects
72, 73, 74, 75, 76, 77, 78, 79, 120, 121
Cave_bureau
80, 81, 82, 83, 84, 85, 86, 87
Ensamble Studio
88, 89, 90, 91, 92, 93, 94, 95
Harrison Atelier
96, 97
Alexandra Daisy Ginsberg / Neues Museum Nuremberg (Annette Kradisch)
98, 99, 100, 101
Alexandra Daisy Ginsberg
102, 104, 107
Joyce Hwang
103, 105, 106
Ants of the Prairie
108, 109, 110, 111, 112, 113
Walter Hood
114, 115
Uncertainty Network Office (UN-Office)
116
Nico Alexandroff